INDIANOMIX

MAKING SENSE OF MODERN INDIA

VIVEK DEHEJIA &
RUPA SUBRAMANYA

PENGUIN BOOKS
An imprint of Penguin Random House

PENGUIN BOOKS

USA | Canada | UK | Ireland | Australia
New Zealand | India | South Africa | China | Singapore

Penguin Books is part of the Penguin Random House group of companies whose addresses can be found at global.penguinrandomhouse.com

Published by Penguin Random House India Pvt. Ltd
4th Floor, Capital Tower 1, MG Road,
Gurugram 122 002, Haryana, India

Penguin Random House India

First published in hardback by Random House India in 2012
Paperback edition published in 2015
This edition published in Penguin Books by Penguin Random House India 2020

10 9 8 7 6 5 4 3 2

The views and opinions expressed in this book are the author's own and the facts are as reported by them which have been verified to the extent possible, and the publishers are not in any way liable for the same

ISBN 9788184006544

Typeset in Sabon by R. Ajith Kumar

Printed at Repro India Limited

www.penguin.co.in

FSC www.fsc.org MIX Paper from responsible sources FSC® C047271

This is a legitimate digitally printed version of the book and therefore might not have certain extra finishing on the cover.

In memory of Pa and Shobha akka,
who both left this world far too soon

PRAISE FOR INDIANOMIX

'Succinctly explains Indian reality in an unconventional manner. The authors use everyday examples to explain complex problems. A riveting read, indeed'—Jay Panda

'This is economics and game theory as great entertainment!' —Gurcharan Das

'Anyone who thought economists were dull people won't do so after reading this book. [It] holds the reader's attention like a Sherlock Holmes mystery'—Arvind Panagariya

'A quirky, thoughtful little book that is sometimes provocative, often surprising and always interesting'—Shashi Tharoor

'A book which must certainly be read by anyone wanting to know what Indians are really about'—Pavan K. Varma

'*Indianomix* teaches you things you never knew, and makes you question the things you thought you knew well. An unusual, enjoyable India book'—Barkha Dutt

'Economics needn't be boring. Economics can be real, not abstract and esoteric. This is a delightful book, illustrating how and why economists look at things. It isn't just about India, it is also about how economics works'—Bibek Debroy

'Manages to keep even the most economic-layman interested . . . cutting-edge and deep research offers a refreshing outlook . . . well-researched and easy to read book that will be adored by laymen who are not familiar with economics'—*Asian Age*

'Coherently brings together a host of research to help the reader make more sense of the world'—*Business Today*

'Fun reading . . . brings to the fore cutting-edge research in the fields of behavioural economics and experimental economics . . . and applies insights from them to understand several vexed real world problems'—*India Today*

'An essential read for those interested in the convergence of economics and psychology . . . a little gem of a book' —*Sunday Guardian*

'[A] delightful book . . . a quintessentially Indian book that opens a window into India – what makes it tick, what makes it err, what makes it success, what makes it gamble – literally and figuratively. What makes the book so remarkable is that besides being a quirky introduction to India, it also doubles as a quirky introduction to economic theory. In the best traditions of reading, *Indianomix* is just never dull'—*Tehelka*

Contents

Introduction: Mind Games

I

Whoever coined the expression 'time waits for no man' obviously never lived in India. Let's face it: except for rocket launches by our world-class space programme, that require coordination down to the last second, we Indians are notorious for our lack of punctuality. India has one time zone, five and a half hours ahead of Greenwich Mean Time (GMT). It's known as Indian Standard Time or 'IST' for short. But in Indian slang, IST has an alternate meaning: 'Indian Stretchable Time'. And some everyday Indian situations would certainly confirm that second meaning. You might invite people home for dinner at 8 p.m. but more than likely, they probably won't show up until 10 or 10.30 by which time you might be half asleep. (In fact, by now, we've perfected a system where between 8 and 10 we have a snack, take a refreshing nap, and are ready for our guests when they eventually arrive.) Our guests might be in flagrant violation of the official IST but are well within the bounds of the unofficial one.

We were acutely reminded of this difference between official and unofficial timings when we returned to India after several years in punctual, Protestant North America. We'd make an appointment with someone, say to meet over coffee at 12 noon, and we would naïvely show up at the stroke of 12 p.m. The other party wouldn't be there. Then, usually around 12.30, we'd get a text saying that they were running late and would be with us 'soon'. That would often stretch into another half hour.

Indeed, so engrained is the culture of tardiness in India, that it's even led to a fashion statement. In 2011, Alok Nanda and Prasanna Sankhe launched the 'ISH' (as in '-ish') watch, inspired by Indian Stretchable Time. Designed by Sankhe, the watch doesn't feature the regularly spaced markings on the face representing hours or minutes. Rather, it's got four markings, '12-ish', '3-ish', '6-ish', and '9-ish', and that, too, not placed exactly where they belong on the dial, but each one displaced to the right a little bit. Looking at the face of the watch, you can, roughly, tell what time it is, but you wouldn't use it to time a rocket launch, which is the point of Sankhe's cheeky design. Sankhe told us that the watch has been selling magnificently well, and has even caught on abroad, as a fashion statement by those for whom being exactly on time isn't necessary or, indeed, might be unfashionable.

Are punctuality, and its flip side, tardiness, cultural traits? You might certainly be forgiven for thinking that if you live in India and everyone else is perennially running late. In this stylized view of the world, there are punctual cultures, those of Protestant Northern Europe and North America, for example, and there are tardy cultures, such as India or Latin America.

Superficially appealing though this chronometric division of the world is, you have to wonder whether punctuality or its absence are as fundamental as deeply rooted beliefs and values. Why really do Indians run late? Economics can help us understand.

Eminent Indian economics professor Kaushik Basu and his collaborator Jörgen Weibull have a subtler and more nuanced take on the question of punctuality than the usual cultural stereotype. Basu is an economics professor at Cornell University, and for three years, until the middle of 2012, was chief economic adviser to the government of India. At the time of writing in 2012, he had just taken up a position as chief economist of the World Bank in Washington, DC. They make the argument that 'while the importance of culture is undeniable, the innateness of culture is not'. What they mean is that traits like punctuality or tardiness might describe a particular culture, such as Indian, but they aren't necessarily deep features. To the contrary, they may reflect human choice as much as history or culture. The armchair psychologist or sociologist might assume that tardiness is just part of being Indian, but the economist has other ideas.

Think about the punctuality problem this way by revisiting our earlier example. When we and our friend decide to meet at 12 noon, suppose both sets of parties believe that everyone indeed will show up at 12 noon. In that case, it would be both in our interest and our friend's interest, in fact, to show up at 12. Suppose, instead, both we and our friend believe that an appointment to meet at 12 noon really means that you should show up closer to 1 p.m. In that case, it would make sense for both us and our friend to show up at 1 p.m. In economic jargon, the problem of meeting someone involves coordination, and this in turn creates the possibility for what economists call 'multiple equilibria'. In plain English that means that meeting at 12 noon or meeting at 1 p.m. are both valid solutions to the 'game' that we and our friend are playing when deciding when to show up. In fact, there's a third equilibrium, in which both we and our friend toss a coin and decide whether to go at 12 noon or 1 p.m., so on 'average' we're meeting at 12.30 if we play the game repeatedly. In game theory jargon, this is an equilibrium in 'mixed' rather than 'pure' strategies.

Multiple equilibria means different ways of life can happily co-exist in the world. That's why Indians drive on the left and Americans drive on the right or why most of the world uses metric measurement while America still uses the old English system, and all of these can exist in harmony. With driving, India has stuck to the system we inherited from the British, with the driver seated on the right side of the car and driving on the left side of the road. A few other countries follow the same system. In the rest of the world, however, including America, the pattern is reversed, with the driver on the left in the right lane. Each set of people intuitively understands that there's a social convention—you can call it culture—on which side of the road to drive on. What's more, it's backed up by the sanction of the law. Both equilibria can co-exist on our planet without any problem at all. And in the event someone crosses from one equilibrium to the other, like an American moving to India, they'll quickly figure out on peril of getting into an accident, which side of the road to drive on.

Have you ever tried to palm off a torn currency note on an unsuspecting shopkeeper in India? If you have succeeded, kudos to you; we've never managed the feat. In some countries, such as the US or Canada, torn currency notes that are taped together are accepted by social convention and can be used in transactions, and this is just fine as everyone shares this convention. In India, by contrast, torn notes aren't generally accepted, and people who hold them need to exchange them at a bank; again, because everyone shares this convention, it works just fine (except for the slight nuisance of going to the bank now and again to trade in torn notes). Here's multiple equilibria once again.

There's one important difference, however, between punctuality or tardiness on the one hand and which side of the road you drive on on the other. In the driving case, it doesn't matter which equilibrium, the left or right side of the road, a society (with all of its rules and institutions) picks, or somehow settles on. What matters is that everyone sticks to it, but either one is equally good. But being punctual is clearly superior to being tardy: one equilibrium is better for society than the other. We'd all be better off if everyone, in fact, were punctual, since we'd all waste a whole lot less time that way. But it's not easy to switch, since there's little payoff for any one individual to deviate from the social norm. If everyone's showing up an hour late and you're the only person showing up on time, you end up the loser. And if everyone realizes this, no one individual has an incentive to switch. This is an example of what economists call a 'coordination failure' or a problem of 'collective action'. It's a bit like why the sidewalk in your neighbourhood is probably filthy if you live in a major Indian city. If everyone is littering, there's no incentive for you to play nice because even if you use the garbage cans or clean up after your pet, the sidewalk will still be dirty. It might sound prosaic, but the answer is coordination failure, not the usual claim that cleanliness isn't part of our culture. After all, the great cities of the West, which are now exemplars of public hygiene, were once as filthy as Indian cities are now. It wasn't culture, but the rule of law solving a collective action problem, that cleaned up London and New York.

Of course, we shouldn't think that following a particular cultural norm is a monolithic feature of a culture. And people who move from a society in one equilibrium to a society in another can and do switch—indeed, they may have no choice but to switch to survive in their new environment. In our case, after a while being back in India, we automatically adjusted ourselves to the local norm and would routinely arrive late ourselves, except that now we were 'really' on time: no more annoying waits for people who were late by the punctual norm but 'on time' by the tardy one.

There's another sense in which cultural norms aren't monolithic. Often, within a larger culture, there are subcultures which will adhere to a different social norm. In India for example, where tardiness is the norm, television programmes still begin on time. And sometimes people or organizations will deliberately try to buck the trend. Indigo, at the time of writing this the leading low-cost airline in India, modelled on the US Southwest Airlines, has on-time departure and arrival as their main goal and they do a great job delivering it: the popularity of the airline (the only Indian airline that actually turned a profit as of 2012) suggests that, when they fly, people are expressing a preference for 'switching', at least temporarily, from the tardy to the punctual equilibrium. Or take an example in reverse. Among the Indian diaspora in North America, cultural events organized by the community will invariably start late, not at the time printed in the announcement that's tacked on the bulletin board of your local Indian grocery store. Members of the community realize that the tardy equilibrium is the one in force. Yet, these same people will go to work on time the next morning, reverting to the punctual Protestant equilibrium.

One important question that the coordination theory of punctuality leaves unanswered is why a particular society ends up fixed on one equilibrium or the other. Why is India fixed on the tardy equilibrium and not the punctual one? Now that could truly be a matter of historical accident or have some sort of cultural antecedent. A classic example of historical accident fixing one out of potentially thousands of equilibria is the standard computer keyboard which has the keys 'QWERTY' in the upper left-hand corner. It turns out that this is what worked best on a typewriter given the position of the metal keys as they struck the paper, not for the ease of the typist, and yet that arrangement has stuck. As a cultural antecedent, for example, a religion which prescribes mandatory worship at a fixed time of the day might be more likely to fix on the punctual equilibrium than a religion which allows a worshipper to pray at any time of the day. Yet, once a society has ended up settling on one or the other, it's very hard to break away, especially in the absence of a wrenching change to the underlying incentives. If it becomes very costly for Indian society to always run late, we may end up switching over time towards being more punctual. Psychology can offer yet another clue as to why cultural traits such as punctuality or tardiness tend to be slow to evolve. Once you've got used to be being late, for example, it involves an effort of will and perhaps a cognitive dissonance to make sure you show up on time, just like it's tough to switch from driving on one side of the road to driving on the other when you move between countries. What history might have decided by the toss of a coin gets engrained through habit and locked in through coordination. That's why Indians run late, and that's the power of economics in action.

II

If running late is common in India, so too, is having your fare refused by a taxi or autorickshaw driver. In Mumbai at least, someone's on your side. The city newspaper *Mid-Day*, in cooperation with the traffic police, has spearheaded a campaign called 'Meter Down', whose goal is to try get Mumbai's 'errant' autorickshaw drivers to play by the rules. They've got no less a figure than Bollywood celebrity John Abraham as a champion. For Abraham, it's personal. In January 2012, Abraham had his fare refused by an autorickshaw driver who didn't want to take him the relatively short distance from his home at Bandstand to the Taj Land's End hotel, both in the posh Mumbai suburb of Bandra (which is just across the sea link from the centre of town). We've all been there. For those of us who live in major cities around the world, whether it's Mumbai, New York or London, few things can be more frustrating than trying to hail a taxi or an autorickshaw (only in Mumbai, none that we're aware of yet in New York or London) only to have an empty vehicle with its flag in the 'up' or available position whizz right past you. That upturned flag is giving you the proverbial finger. And equally annoying, even if the driver bothers to pull over to the kerb, it's more than likely, at least in Mumbai, that you've had your fare refused as often as not, especially if it's a short one. Abraham can, of course, afford his own chauffeur-driven luxury car as his mode of transport if he so desires, but being raised a good middle-class boy by his own say-so he, like the rest of us, doesn't like (not) being taken for a ride. In Mumbai, as in most cities, it's against the rules for a taxi or an autorickshaw to refuse a fare no matter how short. But of course that doesn't stop it from happening, in Mumbai or anywhere else. In New York City for example, yellow cabs aren't allowed to refuse a fare, and a cabbie could get into trouble with city authorities if they actually pull up to the kerb and then refuse to take a passenger. That's why, if they don't want your fare, they'll just drive past and more than likely, won't even make eye contact with you. That way, if you do manage to make a note of their medallion number and lodge a complaint, the driver can always plausibly claim that they didn't see you at all and so obviously couldn't stop.

Perhaps New York cabbies are making enough money to spurn your modest fare, but how about Mumbai's taxi and autorickshaw drivers? Many of them are so poor that they sleep in their vehicles or on the pavement close to where they've parked for lack of affordable accommodation. Even the shortest fare would earn the driver about 20 rupees. That might be pocket change for you or us but for a poor driver that's real money. Frustrated passengers will often explain this behaviour by arguing that drivers who refuse fares are lazy, irrational, and plain ungrateful. Our friends at Meter Down don't use this language, of course, but in their indignation at the 'errant' behaviour of autorickshaw drivers there's more than a hint of this kind of armchair sociological or cultural explanation.

But how errant is the Mumbai driver who refuses a fare? Let's leave aside the legal issues involved and once again see if economics can help us understand what's going on. From the driver's point of view, there's no cost in an accounting sense in refusing your fare, since there was no transaction and no money changed hands. But there is what economists call the 'opportunity cost' of having foregone the money you would have paid him, which is as real as any accounting cost. Plus, there's the chance (admittedly very small) that the driver could actually get into trouble if you report him and this could cost him if his licence is suspended—which is another sort of opportunity cost. Set against these costs, refusing your fare does confer a benefit to the driver: he can keep rolling in the hopes of getting a better fare.

What, short of blind optimism, might affect a trade-off between a certain loss (missing out on your fare) and a possible future gain (the prospect of a better fare)? Common sense suggests several possibilities, some or all of which could be important at any given place and time. For one thing, if the driver is plying near a hotel or a commercial area, he might expect his next fare to be a longer one, say to the airport or a train station, which would make him less likely to accept your short fare. Secondly, if it's around rush hour and there's a greater demand for rides, he might well conclude that passing up your short fare would be less costly than if he did so at an off-peak hour when he might not get another fare for a while. Thirdly, if it's close to the shift change, the driver might not want to go out of his way to drop you to your destination if you're not en route to where he needs to go to hand off to the next driver, which again would make him less likely to take your fare compared to the middle of the shift. All of these common sense explanations can be perfectly understood through the economist's lens of a cost–benefit analysis.

Most importantly, there's a perennial shortage of taxis and autorickshaws in Mumbai, as there's a shortage of metered cabs in most major cities of the world. That's because taxis and autorickshaws don't ply their trade in a free and competitive market but rather, need to be licensed by municipal authorities, who are tight-fisted with the number of permits they issue. In turn, a general shortage of taxis and autorickshaws will mean that there's always going to be another fare around the corner, which makes it less costly for a driver to pass you up. There's a general principle of economics at work here: in a situation of shortage, or 'excess demand', as economists call it, sellers of a product or providers of a service that's in short supply have the upper hand over would-be buyers. (That also helps to explain the shortage in the first place, since it benefits incumbent drivers.) A Mumbai autorickshaw driver thumbing his nose at you is no different in terms of its fundamental economics from the near impossibility of finding a family doctor in a country with socialized medicine, such as Canada—the only difference is that a family doctor usually makes a one-time decision on whether to accept new patients or not whereas a Mumbai autorickshaw driver is deciding every few minutes whether or not to take a fare. The more basic point is whether a well-to-do Canadian doctor or a poor Mumbai autorickshaw driver, the fundamental economic trade-off is the same in both situations.

In effect, the driver's doing to you what you've probably experienced many times in your love life. Every time you've dated someone for a while and then moved on because that person wasn't the right one for you, or more painfully still if you've been on the receiving end of 'it's not you, it's me', it's exactly the same situation. The partner making the decision to move on and not 'settling for someone' is giving up a sure thing right now (like the Mumbai driver giving up a short fare) for the uncertain prospect of something even better, say a long airport fare or ending up with Bollywood celebrity Deepika Padukone down the road.

In fact, so important are these kinds of decisions that weigh a choice today against an unknown future that there's a whole branch of mathematics, routinely used by economists, called 'optimal control theory', built to help solve them. The taxi or autorickshaw driver's problem and your dating decisions are even more specific and are both examples of what's known as an 'optimal stopping problem': when do you stop searching and decide to accept a fare or settle down in life? While it doesn't make it to the plot of too many love stories, at least in the special case where you have a fixed number of 'suitors' and you can rank them all from best to worst, there's actually a mathematical formula that tells you that you should reject the first 37 per cent of your pool of candidates and then pick the next one that scores higher than the highest scoring among the first 37 per cent. That should help you do the math and, in case not, solving an equation or two might just determine whether you end up with John or Deepika or a reasonable facsimile thereof.

As for the taxi problem, if the driver does stop at the kerb, Mumbaikars will tell you that the best advice is to just jump in and be suitably vague about where you're going. If he baulks, it ups the ante for him since you're already in the vehicle, can make a note of his licence number and raise a stink, which increases the cost to him of refusing and makes it more likely he'll accept your fare, even if grudgingly.

III

So now we know why cab or autorickshaw drivers might refuse a fare, even if they're driving by empty. Earlier, we saw how coordination and multiple equilibria might explain why Indians are tardy and Americans are punctual. And all the while we explained these everyday phenomena using everyday economics.

But how would you explain the co-existence of punctuality and tardiness within the same group of people from the same culture (and so presumably sharing the same social norms) converging on the same place? In such situations, something else must be going on. It's not coordination or optimal stopping. If you work in an office, you've probably noticed how the most junior people, especially new hires, will show up early, usually hanging around deferentially waiting for their seniors to arrive. As a rule, the more senior you are, the more laid back you'll be when it comes to showing up on time for work or even for a meeting. And you can be sure that the big boss will show up last, usually with flunkies in tow, well after everyone else.

What's going on in this situation isn't a coordination game, it's all about signalling, yet another important concept in economics. The big boss shows up last, and thereby signals his importance; so too with government ministers who drive around town with flashing red lights on their cars and keep an airplane waiting on the tarmac while they board at their leisure, just because they can. Vivek for one, has spent countless hours waiting in the anterooms of Indian ministers' offices. In one instance, a minister made elaborate plans for his next golf game within earshot while Vivek was cooling his heels in the waiting room, almost an hour after the time of his appointment. This was clearly a signal either of the minister's importance, Vivek's unimportance, or a combination of the two. Take dress as another example. Indian politicians invariably wear traditional garb (such as a kurta-pyjama, dhoti, sari, etc.) when in politicking mode. But particularly among the younger generation, they'll often revert to Western wear, whether business suits or jeans and a T-shirt, when they're away from the glare of the cameras. Notable examples include Priyanka Vadra, scion of the Nehru–Gandhi dynasty, and Omar Abdullah, chief minister of Jammu and Kashmir. Priyanka, for example, wears exquisite traditional handloom saris when visiting the family constituencies in Uttar Pradesh, but sports fashionable jeans, T-shirts, and designer wear back in Delhi. Presumably, her dress choice in UP is meant to signal her authenticity to the voters, appearing matronly and demure rather than revealing herself to be the glamorous city girl she could actually be. Likewise, Abdullah wears traditional Kashmiri garb where necessary, but otherwise is known for his snazzy designer suits, ties, and accessories, and has even graced the cover of *GQ*'s Indian edition in December 2009. And let's be honest: we all do this to some extent. How many of us wear traditional Indian clothes when calling on elderly relatives but switch back to our tank tops, short skirts, jeans, and T-shirts once we get back home?

As a matter of economics, signalling arises in a world with imperfect information. Sending a signal is a way of sending out information about yourself, much like your business card or saying that you have an MBA from one or another prestigious business school. And once you start looking around you see examples of signalling everywhere, much more so in a place like India than in the more egalitarian countries of the West. More stringent and finely defined social hierarchies give rise to way more opportunities for signalling than the more monochromatic world of a place like Canada or Scandinavia where most people are in the middle and there's little to be gained by signalling. Generally speaking, the more traditional and hierarchical a society, the more important social signalling will be, because conveying information about your social and economic standing carries a great deal more weight. It's still more important in Britain say than in the US and more important in the US than in Canada, as you move down from the most to the least stratified of otherwise very similar Anglo-Saxon countries. In these places you don't see so much of the brash red-lights style of signalling that is popular in India. It might be as subtle as sporting the right school tie or ring, what part of town you live in, or your accent. Of course those things are also important in India.

Signalling is only one of several different mechanisms that people can use to overcome problems of imperfect information. The way that an economist would see it, your relationship with, say, your domestic help would be that of a 'principal' to an 'agent'. You're the principal who wants to get something done, and your maid is the agent, whom you've hired to do the job. The trouble is that you can only imperfectly monitor your maid's work, so you don't know whether she's working hard or just goofing off. In the archaic term still used by economists, this is the problem of 'moral hazard'. To overcome this problem, your maid could signal that she's working hard by banging the pots and so forth (as our maid does with an impressively high decibel level), but there's also action you could take. For one, you could monitor her more carefully, but that would waste your time and energy. As an alternative, you could try to pay a better wage, in the hopes of attracting more effort from your maid (so overcoming moral hazard) or attracting a higher quality of domestic help—overcoming what economists call 'adverse selection', more popularly known as the 'lemons' problem. A 'lemon', in American slang, is a used car that has a defect known to the seller but not visible to a would-be buyer. Vivek's car, for example, has a slow battery drain that wouldn't be noticed by a buyer but which he himself knows about. This is another form of imperfect information that queers the market, since lemons are competing with good used cars in the same marketplace. Either way, in the jargon of economics, you'd be paying an 'efficiency wage': a wage higher than you need to, and which is specifically intended to elicit better effort or a better worker.

You might think that using concepts like 'moral hazard' and 'adverse selection' to understand how your domestic help operates is a bit like taking a sledgehammer to a pine nut. In fact these very concepts help us understand some of the most important, even epochal, events of recent global economic history. Take the global financial crisis which started in 2007 in the US and from which the world hasn't yet fully recovered as we write this in the middle of 2012. Banks making bad loans they knew they shouldn't have but did anyway because they felt sure they'd be bailed out by regulators is at root a problem of moral hazard. And the proliferation of so-called 'sub-prime' mortgages in the US housing market—loans taken out by people who couldn't really afford to buy a house in the first place—represents a form of adverse selection in the financial market, flooding the pool of otherwise good quality mortgages with these toxic assets. So, believe it or not, the banks lending when they shouldn't, in terms of economic behaviour and incentives, is no different from your maid slacking off on the job; and lots of people who shouldn't have been borrowing entering the housing market is very much like a lot of 'lemons' flooding the market for domestic help, making it tough to tell them apart from the good ones until you try them out.

Sometimes, clues to the large may be found in the small, and the seemingly trivial can help illuminate the monumentally important. That's the power of economics in action, and that's part of what we try to explore in what follows. As we discovered while writing this book, something as apparently simple as trying to flag down a taxi or autorickshaw, once you peel it open, exposes a multitude of economics concepts that help you better understand the inner workings of life and the impulses that lie beneath everything, from the most banal everyday situations to moments of great historical importance. We wanted to understand India as it is actually is, not as some economist, business guru, or policymaker thinks it ought to be. That's why this book isn't figuring out where the stock market is heading, what the Reserve Bank of India's monetary policy stance should be, or giving you a disquisition on the urgent need for second generation economic reforms. Nor for that matter are we going to delve deeply into the problems of poverty, inequality, and social deprivation, all well covered by the many books on the Indian economy that have come before us. In fact, as you will discover, our subject isn't really about the economy of India at all as much as it is applying the methods of economics to understanding India, especially to exploring themes that in our judgement are underexplored by economists.

That's the gap we aim to fill. While in this introductory chapter we've highlighted everyday issues, in the six chapters that follow we'll tackle questions that span past and present, culture and politics, and the large and the small. Have capitalism and the market economy made Indians more apathetic and uncaring? Do seatbelt laws save lives in India? What was the reason for the Bharatiya Janata Party's defeat in 2004? What can explain Jawaharlal Nehru's behaviour in ignoring the Chinese threat in the lead-up to the 1962 war in which China defeated India? These are just a very few of the questions that we address. Borrowing liberally from other disciplines, including history, political science, psychology, sociology, anthropology, evolutionary biology, and even the study of religion, this is not a conventional economics book. It's about trying to better understand the Indian reality the way that a narrowly defined perspective, whether economic or literary for that matter, can't do on its own. This will involve, in more than a few cases, debunking some hoary myths and calling into question bits of musty conventional wisdom about India that have got encrusted on the conventional, received narrative. The richness of India—which to some people may appear as mere messiness—deserves, indeed demands, such an interdisciplinary approach. When you dig below the apparent chaos of India, and get to the deeper mechanisms hidden below the confusing patterns on top, India makes sense after all.

1
A Helping Hand

I

When the forces of Imperial Japan entered the Chinese city of Nanking on December 13, 1937, no one could have anticipated quite how horrific the consequences would be. Nanking (modern Nanjing), one of the most important cities in Chinese history, served as the capital of the Nationalist Government which had overthrown China's last Imperial dynasty. The Japanese occupied the city throughout the war and it wasn't until 1946, after the defeat of Japan, that the Nationalists moved their capital back to Nanking. Finally, in 1949 the city was taken by the Communists, and remains an important provincial capital to this day.

The late American journalist and historian Iris Chang published a definitive, if highly controversial, book about the Japanese occupation in 1997. Named *The Rape of Nanking*, Chang documents in detail some of the war crimes committed by the occupiers. In the midst of this barbarity, some lucky residents of Nanking found an unlikely saviour in the person of John Rabe. As the head of the International Safety Zone in the city, Rabe sheltered and saved the lives of hundreds of thousands of Chinese.

What made Rabe an unlikely hero? Not only was he a German, and not just a Nazi, he was the leader of the Nazi party in Nanking. Far from looking the other way, as an ally of the Japanese might have done, Rabe chose instead to put himself and his family at personal risk to help as many Chinese civilians and unarmed soldiers as he could. So great was John Rabe's heroism and the number of lives he touched that Chang considered him the 'Oskar Schindler of China' in reference to the German businessman credited with saving over a thousand Jews during the Holocaust by employing them in his factories. Stories such as those of Rabe and Schindler are only two of the most well-known episodes of people putting themselves at risk to rescue others. Equally, there are cases of people who choose to look the other way and not intervene in time of great need. The many people who collaborated with the Nazis in occupied countries in Europe cast the bravery of people like Rabe and Schindler in an even sharper relief.

Indeed, a few years after these events, the bloody Partition of British India into the successor states of India and Pakistan witnessed countless episodes of both altruism and apathy. Violence was already on the rise before Partition, but after August 15, 1947, it erupted into something akin to a civil war in the border regions between the two new states. As recounted in a definitive academic history of the period,

The Great Partition: The Making of India and Pakistan, by British historian Yasmin Khan, the violence and barbarism were brutal and on a huge scale. Things were especially bad in the province of Punjab, where internecine warfare raged between Hindus and Sikhs on the one hand and Muslims on the other.

In the midst of this carnage, contemporary observers and historians have recorded cases both of people turning away in apathy and others reaching out to help others. One episode that Khan recounts is typical of the former category. During an attack on a train, when 70 people or more were being killed outside the town of Khurja, the station master refused to assist in the investigation, nor apparently, had he done anything to prevent the killing. But equally there were many episodes of heroic and altruistic acts, from members of all communities. A policeman whose identity is lost to history and is known only as a 'South Asian Schindler' fended off a murderous gang using only his stick and saved 200 Sikh lives. As these and many other examples attest, for every person who turned on their neighbour in a border town simmering with Hindu–Muslim tension, there was another who sheltered someone from the other community and saved them from certain death.

Events like the Nanking massacre, the Holocaust, and the Partition were major world events, in which individuals had the opportunity to step up to the plate and help others or choose to walk away instead. But human beings face these kinds of choices every day in far less grand and historically charged circumstances. In fact, many people face such choices on the streets of India, China, or just about everywhere else, every day of every year.

More recently than the historical events we chronicled, on October 20, 2011, in the Mumbai suburb of Andheri (West), as many as 50 people were placed in the uncomfortable spot of deciding whether or not to heed a cry for help. They were witnesses to the brutal killings of two young men, Keenan Santos, 24, and Reuben Fernandes, 29, who were out for dinner with friends. According to news reports, a street altercation with a passerby, who is alleged to have made a lewd pass at Keenan's girlfriend Priyanka Fernandes, escalated into tragedy when Keenan and Reuben were stabbed in the ensuing mêlée.

In the extensive media coverage in the days and weeks following the event, a question that often came up was the apparent fact that there were so many onlookers who did nothing to intervene and allowed the tragedy to unfold. Why was this so? This question haunted Priyanka. As she put it in her own agonized words:

> *When my friends Keenan and Reuben were being stabbed repeatedly, mercilessly, I could see at least 50 eyewitnesses, who stood like stone, unmoving and unmoved, as we screamed for help. Not one came forward to join the fray, to help us fight against a reprehensible crime.*

The tragic nature of the deaths of Keenan and Reuben isn't an anomaly. Scan the metro section of any major Indian daily newspaper and you'll find similar accounts of crimes in progress in plain sight or cries for help going unheeded.

In a cruel coincidence, at just about the same time that Keenan lay dying in a hospital bed in Mumbai, a little girl in Foshan, a city in the province of Guandong, China, lost her battle with severe injuries and succumbed to multiple organ failures, breathing her last few breaths early on the morning of October 21, 2011. The toddler, who had been dubbed 'Little Yueyue', or 'Little Joy', by the Chinese media, had, a week earlier, been struck first by a delivery van, then by a truck, and lay dying on the street. According to news reports, she lay there for seven minutes, as 18 pedestrians walked past and did nothing, not even call for help. It was an old scrap peddler who eventually pulled her out of the street and went looking for the girl's parents.

There was no John Rabe, Oskar Schindler, or South Asian Schindler on the scene in either Mumbai or Foshan.

II

In the middle of the nineteenth century, Charles Darwin had theorized that all life forms evolve according to a principle he called 'natural selection', that is, the 'survival of the fittest'. Darwin pioneered the view that genes are trying to maximize their 'fitness', which they do by reproducing themselves. In simpler terms, an organism that lives long enough will be able to procreate and pass on its genes; one that doesn't, won't be able to. This simple mechanism means that the genes of survivors will keep getting passed down through the generations, while those of non-survivors will eventually disappear. Darwin's theory became the accepted scientific explanation for human evolution by the beginning of the twentieth century.

But there was a potentially fatal flaw in the theory which Darwin himself recognized and for which he failed to find a solution. The fly in the ointment is selflessness and altruism, as seen in both humans and in the animal kingdom. If you help someone else, and put your own life at risk as a result, there's a chance you might not be around to pass on your genes to your offspring. How could this possibly make sense in a world of 'selfish genes'? The idea that genes are maximizing their own fitness or survival, and so are 'selfish', is a popular interpretation of Darwin's ideas by the twentieth-century British biologist Richard Dawkins. It fell to the pugnacious and controversial Dawkins to bring evolutionary biology into the popular consciousness in his best-selling 1976 book, *The Selfish Gene*. Yet, examples of altruism abound.

Take the vampire bat, consigned to evoke visions of Dracula at the jugular for most people. They emerge from caves in the dead of night and hunt for their prey. The vampire bat feeds on warm blood and almost any source will do—whether a bird, a cow, or even a human being. The bat's sonar hones in on the pulsation of a vein, and it stealthily approaches its victim. A pair of sharp teeth bite into the flesh, blood seeps out, and the bat licks it up. Bats can sometimes consume their own weight in blood during the night. While this may make the vampire bat seem a solitary and spiteful creature, in fact one could hardly hope for a better neighbour.

Bats are among the most social of animals. They live in huge colonies inside dark caves, sometimes shared by several thousand at a time. The bat also has a rapid metabolism. Unless it feeds constantly, it can starve to death within 60 hours. This biological fact has caused the evolution of a very unique way for bats to share food. A vampire bat that hasn't managed to find prey on a particular night will start licking under the wings of another member of the community who's been chosen that night for this purpose. The two bats then lock their mouths together and the chosen volunteer vomits warm blood into the other's mouth. If bats didn't operate this way, scientists reckon that almost 80 per cent of adult vampire bats would die every year of starvation.

The existence of altruism remained an unsolved mystery in biology for a century after Darwin. The first attempt to crack this mystery came over a few pints of beer in a London pub in the 1950s. There's a well-known legend that tells of famous British biologist J.B.S. Haldane being asked how far he'd go to save someone else's life. Haldane has an important Indian connection. Later in life, he moved to Kolkata and then on to Bhubaneshwar, even becoming an Indian citizen, turning vegetarian, learning Sanskrit, and wearing Indian clothes. Haldane, a few drinks in, is said to have scribbled numbers on a napkin. He then announced that he'd jump into a river to save two brothers but not one, or eight cousins but not seven. It might sound flippant, but there's a powerful idea underneath Haldane's answer. What he was getting at is that every creature, human or otherwise, shares some of its genes with its nearest kin. So, there might be a basis for helping someone who shares enough of your genes to make it worthwhile.

Haldane's idea can be distilled down into a startlingly simple equation:

$$rB > C$$

This equation was the work, not of Haldane, but of William Hamilton, then a young graduate student in London, who wanted to formalize the drunken insight. He did the math (reams and reams of it, contained in back-to-back scientific papers with enough Greek letters to have impressed a rocket scientist), and this little formula was the result.

The equation, called 'Hamilton's rule', says that altruism will be genetically selected through the 'survival of the fittest' if the benefit (B) of an altruistic action exceeds the cost (C), keeping in mind that the benefit must be multiplied by the degree of 'relatedness' (r) between the two creatures. That's why this theory is often called 'kinship altruism'. Here's an example. You and your sibling (if you have one) share 50 per cent of your genes, so $r = 0.5$. If you were contemplating rescuing your sibling from a dangerous and potentially deadly situation, and you actually behaved according to Hamilton's rule, how much would they have to gain compared to what it would cost you to help? According to the equation, the cost to you would have to be less than half of the benefit to them; or, in other words, they should gain at least twice as much as it costs you to help them. Likewise, first cousins share one-eighth of their genes and so the benefit would have to be eight times as large to make it worthwhile. That explains the logic behind Haldane's off the cuff remark. Hamilton's theory, which he dubbed 'inclusive fitness', can be applied to human behaviour as much as to the animal kingdom that evolutionary biologists mostly study. It's a natural explanation of why people help their close relatives, not just their own kids: it's another way for our selfish genes to reproduce themselves. Of course, this isn't to say that people actually do a mental calculation such as explicitly computing Hamilton's rule before deciding to help someone or not. Rather, looking at the rule can help us understand the deep biological forces we might even be unaware of that might drive us to help in some situations and not others.

But can evolutionary biology explain why people help total strangers, where there's no kin relationship, and so no obvious reason to help? Could there be another biological explanation behind the altruistic deeds of a Rabe or Schindler?

A few years after Hamilton, the American biologist Robert Trivers developed the theory of 'reciprocal altruism', which has been just about as influential as Hamilton's kinship-based theory. According to this alternative (and complementary) theory, if creatures are organized into compact, tightly knit communities, helping a member of the community might make sense because there's a good chance that another member of the community will come to your aid in your time of need. Or there might be such an intricate division of labour within the community that it's likely in each individual organism's own interest to cooperate just to survive. In other words, the existence of cooperative behaviour and the possibility of altruism are closely related.

Consider the leaf-cutter ant. These tiny creatures live in huge colonies in the tropical rainforests of South America. They have an intricate division of labour, divided into seven tasks ranging from cutting leaves to harvesting them to gardening them into fungi that can be consumed. This kind of cooperative behaviour is observed in many species of insects, particularly ants and bees. The trouble is that, like the bats, it's hard to reconcile with purely selfish fitness-maximizing genes. The reason is that a group of opportunistic, selfish organisms could 'invade' a group of cooperative ones, and do better by free riding on them. The cooperators would then be driven to extinction and be replaced by the selfish non-cooperators as the fittest group. Thus a theory like reciprocal altruism could help explain how such cooperation could arise in the natural world.

Trivers' insight applies to human communities as much as it does to colonies of vampire bats, ants, or bees, and suggests yet another reason from evolutionary biology why we might sometimes observe altruistic behaviour among humans as well. The trouble with reciprocal altruism is that it makes sense in small neighbourhoods but doesn't work well as a theory when the number of people gets large. Take life in a modern big city, with a population numbering in the tens of millions or even more, as in the case of India and China. Even sticking to your part of town, your group of 'neighbours' might still easily be as large as a few thousand. Your odds of encountering any one particular neighbour would be tiny, almost zero. Add to that the fact that in a modern city, people are on the move, so your pool of neighbours would change over time. Now, the probability that someone you helped in the past would be able to help you in the future becomes so close to zero you might as well call it a 'fat chance'.

But the generosity of Rabe, Schindler, or the South Asian Schindler, and others like them, remains unexplained by biological theories such as kinship or reciprocal altruism. They weren't saving their kin, nor could they possibly have been expecting reciprocal aid from the desperate people they helped. Even in the Partition, it would be a stretch to suggest that reciprocity was the driving force behind people who helped. These were communities being torn apart and divided into two new states and it was highly unlikely that someone you risked your life for would ever be able to return the favour. We have to account individuals like these as exceptional—as 'outliers', in the language of statistics—exceptions who prove the rule.

The possibility for altruism coming out of kinship or reciprocity is very limited in scope. And when it does exist, it's fragile, and can easily be undone. Some species of insects, for example, have switched from being cooperative to thinking better of it and turning solitary again. Recently, E.O. Wilson, a Harvard biologist and the world's leading expert on insects, has argued that inclusive fitness is, in fact, best understood as a special case of Darwin's original theory of natural selection. In a landmark paper in the scientific journal *Nature* in 2010, Wilson, writing with two mathematician colleagues at Harvard, makes the case. It's erupted into one of the great intellectual battles in evolutionary biology, with Richard Dawkins and most of the profession lined up against the maverick Wilson.

The importance of outliers is that they may condition how we think about a phenomenon. The very fact that the Rabes and Schindlers of the world went against the grain, and exhibited acts of courage and heroism far greater than a conventional theory of altruism can explain is what causes their stories to resonate. Their salience, however, might give us the wrong idea that such altruism is the norm: it's not. In the human world as in the animal kingdom, apathy (or selfishness, more generally), not altruism, appears to be the 'default' setting for many situations. Perhaps Darwin shouldn't have been that worried after all.

III

Evolutionary biology leaves us distinctly pessimistic about the possibility that altruism can arise naturally among humans. What about economics? There's a curious parallel between the way that economists look at altruism and the way that biologists look at it. Biologists for the most part study the animal kingdom, and economists the world of human beings, but, for both, there's a basic paradox to explain. For the biologists, the problem is fitting altruism into a framework driven by selfish genes. For economists, who are used to thinking about humans as rational, self-interested 'maximizers', there's the identical problem.Traditionally, economists have dodged this problem by assuming that, for whatever reason, most people do have at least a small altruistic impulse, even though they're mostly selfish. There is a sophisticated new literature at the intersection of economics and biology, which constructs mathematical models to show how altruism may arise through natural selection. These build on the original insight of Hamilton's rule but extend it to a much richer and complicated environment. The bottom line here, too, is that altruism is likely to arise under special circumstances and cannot be assumed to arise in many or all cases. In the jargon of economics, if altruism exists, people are said to have 'social preferences', that is, preferences which aren't just self-regarding but consider the welfare of others as well. Evolutionary biology could once again come to the rescue. Recent research based on the idea of 'group selection'—rather than natural selection at the level of the individual organism—suggests that altruism might be genetically selected if it helps a group survive compared to other groups in which everyone is purely selfish. This theory, controversial within biology circles, has been championed by the ever iconoclastic E.O. Wilson. This social preferences approach started with the pioneering work of Economics Nobel Laureate Gary Becker of the University of Chicago, and was carried on by other Chicago economists such as Richard Posner and William Landes.

While they can't explain the origin of altruism, economists working in this tradition have tried to capture the trade-offs someone might face in deciding whether to be altruistic. In deciding whether to help someone in need, a would-be rescuer is going to compare the benefits to the person in need along with the costs to themselves, and weigh those somehow. In a way, it's not that different from an economist's version of Hamilton's rule.

First, the cost of rescuing someone could be much higher than, say, just shouting at them from across the street. Suppose you see a streetside brawl breaking out. If you decide to intervene, there might be a real danger that you could be injured or killed yourself. In the case of Keenan and Reuben, for a passerby to jump in might have involved mixing it up with assailants bearing weapons and there'd be a fair chance of getting injured yourself.

Second, if you do help, your victim, ironically, might really jack up your costs of helping. You're probably not expecting a medal, but you'd hope that the person you rescued doesn't turn around and accuse you of being the perp. Yet this is exactly what happened in some well publicized incidents where would-be rescuers were thanked for their pains by being stuck with costly hospital bills they shouldn't have paid, a lawsuit, being harassed by the cops, or even time in the slammer. In China, the most famous case is that of Peng Yu, a student who helped an elderly lady who'd fallen onto the ground after getting off a bus. He helped get her to the hospital and even paid her bill, but in return she sued him and blamed him for the fall. In a now infamous verdict, the judge ruled in her favour, arguing that you'd only help a stranger in need if you had a guilty conscience! In India, we've all heard of such situations in which people are reluctant to intervene, such as when an accident has happened. This additional potential headache is a cost most people probably wouldn't want to bear.

Then again, costs aren't always tangible. For economists, some of the most important costs are invisible and don't appear on any balance sheet: 'opportunity costs'. Invisible they may be, but magical they're not. As the term implies, these are the costs implicitly borne by doing one thing when you might have done something else instead. For example, if you spend your own savings to start a business, you aren't paying the interest on a loan, but you're forgoing the interest you could have earned by keeping the money in the bank. The most important opportunity cost is often time. In a situation of potential rescue, chances are you'll spend a couple of hours or even more of your time. It's not always as simple as making a phone call. You may need to follow up and file a report with the police or other authorities. That would be time spent away from something else you might rather be doing, whether work or leisure. It's noteworthy that Little Yueyue was eventually rescued by an elderly woman who was a scrap peddler in the area and presumably had some time on her hands and not much to lose, not by a high-powered investment banker who shelved an important deal in order to rescue a little girl.

What's more, the 'costs' of helping aren't always even strictly economic—they may be psychological costs that make it more difficult to help. In a very famous psychology experiment, John Darley and Daniel Batson signed up students at a religious seminary to give a practice sermon on, ironically enough, the Good Samaritan parable. Half the students were told that they were ahead of schedule, while the other half were convinced that they were running late. On the way to giving the talk, all of them passed by an actor hired by the researchers. He looked injured, was slumped in a doorway, and was moaning and coughing. While the majority of test subjects who thought they had extra time stopped to help, only 10 per cent of those who thought they were late, did the same, such was their haste to speak on the virtue of helping those in need in a timely manner. In the context of chaotic and stressful daily lives in India or China, it's not hard to see how the kinds of psychological stresses that Darley and Batson uncovered are likely to be at work.

The higher the costs, the less likely it is for people to help, and the higher the chances that people will opt not to help others in need. If this is a situation society doesn't like, it's possible for governments to intervene. One major form that intervention might take is legislation: a law that requires someone to do something or prohibits them from doing something else.

IV

There used to be a time, not that long ago, when non-smokers felt like a beleaguered majority. Smokers seemed to rule the roost, whether it was the office, a bar, or restaurant, or worst of all, in the confines of an airplane. It was almost impossible to find a non-smoking bar or restaurant, leaving non-smokers who loathed second-hand smoke little choice but to stay at home. But over time, as science uncovered the damaging effects of smoke not just on your own health but on people around you, non-smokers became more militant in asserting their rights to smoke-free air and one after another, governments around the world began to intervene.

If there are in fact enough non-smokers out there, you'd think that the market would respond to this need and non-smoking bars and restaurants would spring up without government intervention. But for the most part they didn't. One possible reason is that the economics of bars and restaurants favoured smokers over non-smokers. These places make most of their money from selling drinks, not food. A bottle of wine, for example, could be marked up four or five times or even more its market price. Smoking and drinking at bars tends to be correlated, with even people who consider themselves non-smokers smoking 'socially' while they are drinking.

So you can see why a bar or restaurant wouldn't want to go non-smoking and turn away people contributing to a large part of its revenue.

Another possible reason is what economists call a 'coordination failure'. Suppose a bar owner wants to go non-smoking because they think it's the right thing to do. If they could persuade all of the nearby bars to also go non-smoking, they could manage to do it without losing much business—smokers would have to butt out or go much further afield to find a bar where they could smoke. But there's always the possibility that one of the nearby bars might renege on the agreement and allow smoking. Our well-intentioned bar owner would likely follow suit to avoid losing most of their business. This type of coordination failure is often called a 'Prisoners' Dilemma', inspired by an example from game theory, the branch of mathematics which studies strategic interactions. A third reason may be simpler and more directly commercial: bars used to rely on tobacco sales, and the advertising that tobacco companies paid for, to supplement their income from selling food and drink. Kicking out the smokers would cut off this additional source of money. For instance, in bars in Germany until fairly recently, tobacco company 'representatives' (usually scantily clad women) would ply customers with free samples of cigarettes and no doubt paid the bar owner for the privilege of doing so.

In most countries it took government-imposed bans before bars and restaurants went non-smoking. In India, such a nationwide ban, which in fact covered all public places, came into effect on October 2, 2008. Despite initial scepticism about enforcement, the law has in fact been strikingly successful at least in the major cities like Mumbai or Delhi; hotels, bars, and restaurants strictly enforce the smoking ban in enclosed spaces, although smokers can still find some comfort in open-air smoking areas.

So what does the smoking ban have to do with altruism or helping someone in need?

In the old days before the smoking ban, smokers after all, had the option not to light up. Suppose you were a smoker seated at a bar surrounded mostly by non-smokers. If you were driven by your altruistic impulses, you might have opted not to smoke. That might well have happened on numerous occasions in various bars and restaurants. But obviously this wasn't a strong enough force for all of the smokers to refrain from indulging in their habit when surrounded by non-smokers. This yet again reinforces the idea that altruism seems to be as hard to come by among humans as among animals, and apathy seems to be the norm.

We've seen how both evolutionary biologists and economists study the existence or absence of altruism. Both perspectives suggest that altruism is likely to be a scarce and fragile commodity. If everyone is looking out only for themselves, why would we see anyone like a John Rabe or Oskar Schindler, putting themselves at risk helping others? Everyone would behave like the individuals in Mumbai or Foshan who didn't help.

But is relying on altruism of some sort the only way to guard yourself against the apathy of others? Even in a world in which everyone's selfish, people protect themselves from catastrophes, at least to some extent, by taking out insurance. You pay a small premium up-front with the benefit of receiving help (financial or otherwise) if the bad possibility you insured yourself against actually materializes. That's how house or car insurance works. The trouble is there are many situations in life in which the contingencies are so complicated, and difficult to predict, that insurance simply isn't available. There's no insurance plan in the world that would have protected Keenan and Reuben from being attacked or Little Yueyue from being struck on the street. And even if you have car insurance, all that gives you is collision or liability coverage; it obviously won't guarantee that someone will come to your aid in the event of a road accident.

This is a classic case of what economists call a 'market failure'. The existence of a market failure is one of the most important arguments economists make for government intervention in the free market, albeit reluctantly if you belong to the 'Chicago School'. The 'Chicago School' refers to economists associated with the University of Chicago, who generally are supportive of markets and sceptical of government intervention to fix market failures. What economists in the Chicago tradition would argue is that any potential benefits of a law or regulation must be weighed against the costs of implementing it, the possibility that it's done so with error, and the chance that the law or regulation may be 'captured' by interest groups or through 'rent-seeking' or otherwise have unintended consequences that negate its impact. In other words, the evident fact of market failure must be compared against the possible likelihood of 'government failure' before deciding on whether it makes sense to intervene or leave the market to sort itself out: if the possible government failure is costlier for society than the original market failure, it would be better to do nothing.

In the case of insurance against being attacked on the street or being struck by a vehicle, the market failure is 'catastrophic': the market simply doesn't exist. And the reason for that is what are known as 'transaction costs'. In economic jargon, these are specifically those costs involved in negotiating a deal, making a trade, taking out insurance, printing a menu, shipping a product by sea, or basically engaging in any economic transaction. These are costs distinct from what we usually think of as the cost of doing business, which involves things like paying wages, interest on a bank loan and so on. Think of transaction costs as dust thrown into a microscope: you can still see through it, but not as well as you could before. They are at the root of market failure.

It contains the answer to the seeming paradox of why non-smoking bars didn't come up on their own, saving the government the need to step in and ban smoking. There's a demand for non-smoking bars, but a supply isn't forthcoming. And the deeper reason may lie in transaction costs. Suppose all of the non-smokers in a city could band together and take a united front, saying that they wouldn't patronize a bar or restaurant that allowed smoking. Then, a few bars and restaurants might find it worth their while to switch and become non-smoking. But imagine the transaction costs involved in striking such a deal, and the difficulty involved in enforcing it? They'd be impossibly high, and the market failure would persist.

The rescue situation is analogous. Imagine the complexity of negotiating in advance with everyone who could possibly be on the scene to help out, at the precise moment and at the precise time when you need help. You don't have to think about it for more than a second to realize how impossibly high the costs of figuring all of this out would be, to say nothing of striking separate deals with all of your possible rescuers. The upshot is that, in most situations of rescue, the market isn't going to solve the problem, and we're going to have to rely on altruism, no matter how imperfect, when people are in need. But altruism could use a helping hand.

V

Piyush Tewari knows better than most the tragic effects of human apathy. On April 5, 2007, at about 3.30 p.m., young Shivam Bajpai was walking home from school in the city of Kanpur in the state of Uttar Pradesh. He was hit by a vehicle and fell onto the road. A few minutes later, he was run over by another vehicle. Somehow, young Shivam mustered the strength to drag himself to the side of the road and under the shelter of a tree. He lay bleeding there while several hundred passersby ignored his plight and left him. About 45 minutes after he was first struck, the last drop of life bled out of him as people watched. It was his sixteenth birthday.

For his family, it was a double blow. Shivam's father had passed away when Shivam was only six months old. He'd been raised by his cousin, Piyush, who looked after him as if he was his own younger brother. After the tragedy, he spent months unravelling the sequence of events that led to Shivam's senseless and early death. What shocked him most, and really shook him to the core, was the apparent apathy of so many onlookers. He made it his life's mission to prevent such tragedies from happening in future. Piyush had been working for a US-based private equity firm, and in 2008, became the CEO of their India operations. This gave him the resources and the network to create an NGO, Save Life Foundation, devoted to helping victims of roadside accidents in India. In May 2011, he quit his job to devote himself fully to the work of his NGO.

The problem that Save Life Foundation is tackling is a big one. On average, 80 per cent of the victims of roadside accidents in India don't receive the emergency treatment they need within the 'golden hour', the first hour after an accident. Some of this is no doubt due to the fact that on India's crowded streets, victims don't make it to an emergency room on time for whatever reason, but this cannot be the whole story.

Piyush figured out very early on that what deters most people in India from helping the victims of roadside accidents is their fear of getting involved with the police. The onlookers he interviewed in Kanpur told him in no uncertain terms *that* was the main reason for not helping his dying cousin. In economic terms, the opportunity cost of getting involved was just too high and overwhelmed whatever altruistic instincts they may have had—it was not the over-used 'bystander effect'. And it certainly wasn't a vague cultural reason sometimes invoked by Indians (or Chinese) themselves to explain why people in India (or China) are apathetic.

Yet, in the immediate aftermath of the tragedies in Mumbai and Foshan, people in both countries decried the apparent apathy of the passersby, and both India and China witnessed a national debate. In a sense, the debates that played out in India and China were an instance of a much older debate on the relationship between capitalism and the market system on the one hand and morality on the other. In fall 2008, the John Templeton Foundation, a philanthropic organization, posed this question as an on-line conversation among global experts drawn from different backgrounds and walks of life. Pointedly, the topic for debate was framed thus: 'Does the free market corrode moral character?' Interestingly, many of the non-economists among the experts certainly seemed to think so.

In China, after the Foshan tragedy, some went so far as to blame Mao's Cultural Revolution and the nature of Chinese culture itself, as well as the transformation that had been caused by the lusty embrace of free markets, capitalism, and globalization. Meanwhile back in India, in newspapers, on television talk shows, and in the social media, commentators sounded an eerily similar theme, echoing an alarm that is often raised in India: blaming the tragedy of Keenan and Reuben on the breakdown of morals and values, suggesting that things hadn't been like this in earlier times, when community values were more important than self-seeking and money-making in the consumer culture of the liberalized Indian economy.

But the experience of Piyush and his NGO calls into

question such simplistic cultural arguments and puts the focus back on the incentives to help or to turn away. That's why a key part of his NGO's strategy is to empower local volunteers who've been vetted and nominated by the police. This way, there would be little or no danger that they would end up being harassed by the cops if they tried to help an accident victim.

Starting with a pilot project in Delhi and a second in rural Maharashtra, the foundation trains these volunteers in the basics of roadside accident assistance and life support, interventions like how to stop bleeding, administering CPR, and how to immobilize the neck and spine to prevent paralysis. The volunteers would be contacted by a central call centre, which in turn could be alerted that an accident has happened through a toll free number that's publicized through the media and, for instance, through flyers handed out at the toll gates of expressways.

In the Delhi pilot project, at the time we spoke to Piyush, the plan was to mobilize 8,000 volunteers, 50 to each of the 160 police precincts in the most accident-prone parts of the city, often close to highways. These volunteers are drawn from all walks of life, but it's vital that they're local to the area and are mobile, so they can respond in a timely way to an emergency. They run the gamut from doctors in the neighbourhood to students, roadside hawkers, shopkeepers, and everyone in between.

Volunteers don't receive any monetary reward for being available to help; at the most they'll get minor expenses reimbursed, like the cost of the first aid kits that they carry. Piyush stresses that a big part of the appeal for potential volunteers to sign up is their recognition as 'local heroes'.

They're issued a card which identifies them as volunteers and their work is recognized through media events at which, for example, they get their pictures in the paper.

So is being motivated to help because you're looking for recognition altruism or self-interest? It lies somewhere in between, like the kinship or reciprocal altruism that the biologists talk about. Economists have identified the 'warm glow' of giving as one of the main drivers of charitable contributions. Most large donations, say to museums or universities, are usually associated with the donor's name or their family or a relative who's passed away. Very rarely will you see the 'Gallery of Art in Memory of Anonymous'. Something similar is at work in the recognition that volunteers for Save Life Foundation would receive for their efforts. As Piyush explained to us, the roadside assistance programme is one leg of a three-legged stool. The second is a public awareness campaign to let people know about the dangers posed by roadside accidents and what they can do to help. But the third and most important leg is policy advocacy. Piyush firmly believes that India needs a Good Samaritan law if there's going to be progress on getting people to help out rather than turn away in situations like roadside accidents.

The idea behind such laws is that governments can help to mandate public virtue. Taking a leaf from the Biblical parable, Good Samaritan laws require witnesses to, say, a roadside accident to offer assistance and protects them from civil liability or criminal prosecution if they do so, except if they're grossly negligent (like if someone dies because after you rescue them you stop for a leisurely meal while they're moaning in pain on the back seat of your car before you finally take them to the hospital). In some Anglo-Saxon or common law jurisdictions, Good Samaritan laws exist at the sub-national level; a number of Canadian provinces and US states have enacted such laws. In civil law jurisdictions such as in Europe or the Canadian province of Quebec, the law enshrines a 'duty to rescue', which has a similar intent.

It's interesting to note that Good Samaritan laws don't show up anywhere in the world before the middle of the nineteenth century. A compelling explanation is that in pre-industrial societies, reciprocal altruism might have done the job, so there was no need to legislate the obligation to rescue someone in need. The Chicago economists William Landes and Richard Posner wryly note the 'suggestive' fact that such laws tended to be adopted early on by Fascist and Communist states. For example, the Napoleonic penal code in France dating from 1810 doesn't have a duty to rescue provision. It first shows up in 1941 when the Nazi-backed Vichy government passed a law requiring citizens both to report would-be criminals and to help people in need. So one day you'd be obliged to save someone and maybe turn them in the next day? One possible reason for this strange fact might be that the value of citizens' time is considered 'public property' in such states more than in individualistic and liberal jurisdictions: hence the greater willingness to impose more obligations on citizens.

So what's the situation in India? As in many other areas, the legal situation for potential rescuers is rather murky. While there's no Good Samaritan law, the Supreme Court has argued that doctors at the scene of an accident should render assistance, and the public in general is encouraged to help out. However, there's no protection offered from criminal prosecution or civil liability in case something goes wrong in the effort to help. (At the time we write this, in July 2012, there is news that the state of Maharashtra may provide incentives to encourage people to render assistance to accident victims. Even if these come into effect though, it's far from being anything as comprehensive as a Good Samaritan law.) As we've seen, those jurisdictions which do have such laws provide these protections, except in cases of gross negligence, exactly to reduce the opportunity cost of someone helping out.

The work of Piyush Tewari and Save Life Foundation shows us that a creative approach to tackling a problem like our apparent apathy to people in need starts with understanding people's incentives. While it's still a work in progress, his early success is convincing evidence that the key to getting more people to help others in distress isn't to bemoan the ill effects of capitalism or globalization, but to take concrete steps to *change* those incentives. People may be largely self-serving, as economists assume, but what altruism they do have won't come to the surface if it's stifled by incentives that stack the deck against trying to help if one can.

With a law enforcement system that protects and doesn't penalize rescuers, and perhaps with some form of a Good Samaritan law (minimally, preventing rescuers from being harassed), there's no reason Indians or Chinese wouldn't behave a bit more altruistically if they had the chance to help someone in need.

2

The Human Factor

I

In the fall of 1962, two great countries, each recently liberated from tyranny, fought a brief and bloody war which was lopsided in the extreme. One country routed and humiliated the other. And as if to punctuate this military triumph, it voluntarily gave up the spoils of victory and unilaterally declared a ceasefire. That war is but a footnote in the history of the victorious country and is a source of continuing angst and introspection among many of the intelligentsia in the losing country.

Historians debate and argue over the causes of India's lack of military preparation and failure to take the Chinese threat seriously. It's as commonplace in living room conversations as it is in academic seminars to lay the blame on Jawaharlal Nehru. Nehru, India's first prime minister, had helped lead the freedom struggle against the British along with Mahatma Gandhi and other leaders of the Indian National Congress.

Equally common is the assertion that it was the defeat in the India–China war that finished Nehru, physically, emotionally, politically, and in the eyes of history. He was to die two years later, and for many commentators his ignominious defeat at the hands of the Chinese has tarnished his legacy as the newly independent country's first leader.

For something as complicated as a war, even a short one, there are many lenses through which you can look at it. Military historians, international relations specialists, policy wonks, and even cultural theorists each have their own take. For the military expert, the analysis is pretty open and shut: India was underprepared and simply overwhelmed by China's superior military prowess, strategy, and tactics. For the specialist in diplomacy, Indian officials had failed to decipher the signals that the Chinese were sending. For the student of culture, this was an epic clash between two great civilizations, each with a rich and proud history and tradition. And for the political theorist, this was a great test of the relative strengths and weaknesses of democracy versus authoritarianism.

For Nehru, the war itself must have been bitterly ironic. He was always sympathetic to China and saw the Chinese as an ally in the battle against imperialism, colonialism, and fascism. Even before independence, at an important conference held in Delhi in 1947, he referred to China as 'that great country to which Asia owes so much and from which so much is expected'. This was at a time when China was still ruled by the Nationalists under Chiang Kai-shek. In 1949, the Communists came to power in China. Unlike some other observers, Nehru didn't see China's turn to communism as problematic for India. Even though border tensions were brewing, he seemed oblivious to the fact that China may lay claim to some territory that India considered its own. In 1952 he said that there wasn't 'the slightest reason' to expect Chinese aggression on the north-eastern frontier. In June 1954, the Chinese leader Zhou-En-Lai visited India, and Nehru received him enthusiastically. He returned the favour and visited China in October 1954. It is said that in Beijing a million people lined the streets to cheer Nehru and Zhou as they drove from the airport to the city centre. As he wrote to his close friend Edwina Mountbatten, he was taken by what he saw as the crowd's 'emotional' reaction to him. In late 1956, Zhou visited India a second time. The Dalai Lama was in his entourage and told Nehru privately that conditions were so bad in Tibet that he wanted to seek exile in India. Nehru advised him to return home, offering no support at that juncture.

Things turned sour in July 1958 when an official Chinese map showed large parts of India as Chinese territory. And it wasn't just on paper: it turned out that the Chinese had built a road linking the provinces of Xinjiang and Tibet, a road which traversed a largely uninhabited portion of the Ladakh region of the Indian state of Jammu and Kashmir. The Chinese told the Indians in no uncertain terms that the boundary drawn by the British between the two countries, known as the 'McMahon line', was an artefact of imperialism and therefore, not legitimate. The Chinese leadership offered their Indian counterparts a pragmatic solution: each side should hang on to the territory that they actually controlled, and leave the legal border to an eventual settlement. For good or ill, that sensible Chinese proposal didn't fly with Nehru or India's political class.

The bilateral relationship was further worsened by the warm reception (a reversal from Nehru's previous lukewarm attitude) that the Dalai Lama received from senior politicians when he fled to India in March 1959 and set up a government in exile within India. The Chinese saw the Indian decision to give him sanctuary and shower so much attention on him as outright treachery. By this time, intermittent clashes were already occurring along the disputed border. Even then, in October 1959, Nehru did not think that Indians 'should get alarmed' at the situation. In 1960, Zhou came to India one last time but the two sides failed to settle the border dispute. Just two years later, war broke out. And as late as August 1961, as recounted in writer and politician Shashi Tharoor's 2003 biography of Nehru, the prime minister told Parliament 'that India did not believe in war', and would not act 'in a huff' but behave with 'wisdom and strength'.

In October 1962, the Chinese mounted a major attack along the disputed border in the east and the Indians were totally overwhelmed. Chinese troops came right down into Assam and as it were within shooting distance of Calcutta (today called Kolkata) in the state of West Bengal. On November 22, the Chinese announced a unilateral ceasefire and withdrew from almost all of the territory that they'd occupied. India's, and Nehru's, humiliation was complete.

Tharoor's harsh but well-reasoned verdict is that, in Nehru's approach to the Chinese, 'self-delusion compounded arrogance'—and *that* from someone who is self-professedly a great admirer of Nehru. And in 2011, in a lecture on Nehru and the 1962 war given at Harvard, noted historian Ramachandra

Guha said that the 'debacle at the hands of China still hangs as a huge cloud over Nehru's reputation'.

After the debacle, Nehru himself admitted:

> *We were living in an artificial atmosphere of our own creation.*

How could Nehru's assessment have been so far off the mark and have changed so radically over a short span of time?

II

Now consider a different kind of assessment that also involves computing the odds of success and deciding your course of action accordingly.

In March 2012, the American lottery called 'Mega Millions' had amassed a jackpot worth a staggering $640 million, the largest in history to that point. In the frenzied few days before the draw, over a billion tickets were sold: that's the equivalent of more than three tickets per man, woman, and child in the US. In the state of New York, 1.3 million tickets were being sold—that's per hour!

But what were the odds of winning? It was just one in 176 million. Let's put this number in perspective. In another well-publicized national lottery, this time in Canada, the odds of buying the winning ticket was one in about 14 million. That's much better odds than Mega Millions. But consider that you're more likely to be struck by lightning (in the US, one in about 280 thousand in a given year), killed by a terrorist while travelling (one in 650 thousand), or die of a flesh-eating disease (one in a million). Likewise, playing a casino game like baccarat or roulette has negative odds: if you play long enough, the house will always win. In American-style roulette, for example, the 'house edge' is a hefty 5.4 per cent, while in the slightly fairer European version, it's still around 3 per cent. It's like putting your money in a bank account that withdraws 3 or 5 per cent of it every month! Knowing that fact doesn't keep the gamblers away. Vivek discovered this the hard way, although he had the satisfaction of becoming a rated player at the Las Vegas Hilton and enjoying many of the other blandishments that Sin City has to offer. One tip: If you must gamble, stick to baccarat, which has about the fairest odds you'll get—a little more than a 1 per cent house edge for either the 'player' or 'banker' bet. Only suckers bet on the 'tie'. We urge you not to pursue this research too far lest you, too, become a rated player at the Las Vegas Hilton some day.

All of these people rushing to buy tickets or playing the tables would have done better by just keeping their money under the mattress and even better by putting it into a bank account. Given these poor odds, it's not surprising that a conventional economist will tell you it never makes sense to buy a lottery ticket or gamble in a casino: anyone doing so would be deemed irrational. Such an economist looks at buying a lottery ticket, or for that matter most decisions an individual has to consider, by comparing the benefits and the costs to see if it's worth doing. For most lotteries, like the two we've seen, your chances of winning are so tiny that it never makes sense to pay the purchase price of a ticket no matter how big the possible winnings. Likewise, casino gambling has a negative payoff since the odds are stacked against you: again, it's irrational from the point of view of conventional economics.

Yet, every year, millions of people gamble their money in casinos from Las Vegas to Macau and millions more continue to buy lottery tickets. And that makes the casino magnates very rich, as well as bringing in a lot of revenue for perennially cash-strapped governments the world over. In India too, lotteries are big business. They're legal in only 12 states and five Union Territories but in other states there's a thriving illicit market in lottery tickets which might be sold by a local chaiwallah (streetside tea vendor) or news and cigarette stands. While it's tough to measure the value of a business that's illegal in so many states, according to at least one report, sales of lottery tickets earn a staggering $26 billion.

It's one thing for governments to rake in money from selling lottery tickets, but what if the cops enticed you into a lottery that would pay you for not breaking the law?

Yet, this is exactly what happened in Delhi in January 2012. As part of the 'Road Safety Week', the Delhi police came up with a novel plan to improve pedestrian safety. They would issue coupons to people who crossed major intersections using 'FOBs' or foot overbridges, entering them into a draw to win a prize of 5,000 rupees. Many pedestrians don't use the FOBs, and instead cross illegally—and dangerously—on the road surface. In 2010, there were over 500 pedestrian deaths in Delhi, making it one of the most unsafe cities in India for pedestrians. And in the most recent government report, from 2011, the number of pedestrians killed in road accidents in Delhi had jumped to 935.

The idea of paying people to follow the law isn't as wacky as it sounds. The cops seem to understand that the element of chance is what may just make the scheme work. In the first two weeks of the lottery, police officers were giving out the coupons outside the Income Tax Office at Pragati Maidan and in Anand Vihar, both busy crossing points. For the second phase the police declined to say where they'd be handing out the coupons. This time they were even going to remember to write down the names and numbers of the people getting the coupons. (You have to wonder why, in the first phase, anyone would bother to collect a lottery ticket if there was no way for the cops to contact you and tell you that you'd won. Now that is typically Indian!) The police commissioner in charge of traffic told journalists that announcing in advance where the coupons would be given out would 'defeat the purpose' since people would congregate there. Just like the casinos, the Delhi police had a lot of takers, giving away almost 20,000 coupons in the first weeks of the scheme. And people 'gamble' in other ways all the time, like crossing a dangerous intersection on the surface rather than walking to an FOB where it's safe to cross. The Delhi police were hoping they'd take a gamble on the coupon rather than a gamble on their lives.

III

Now consider a much riskier gamble than buying a lottery ticket. Mumbai is a teardrop-shaped peninsula that's attached to the mainland of Maharashtra. It's wide at the top and narrows down to a point at its southern tip. That peculiar geography helps explain a strange feature of Mumbai's transportation corridors, as the map illustrates. There are two main commuter train lines, the Western and the Central, and a few smaller lines, all of which start at the narrow south and work their way north. The Western line hugs the coast, but the trouble is with the Central, which cuts a big chunk of Mumbai in half. For almost a 60-kilometre distance, there are very few places a pedestrian can cross the Central line. This creates a real challenge for folks who live on one side but need to get to work or school on the other. Think of it as a slightly less extreme version of the Berlin Wall.

If you can afford it, you can get around this by taking a private car, taxi, or an autorickshaw. But for many of the city's poor, that simply isn't an affordable option. Most of the city's poor, or a staggering half of the population of Mumbai, live in slums. These often abut the railway line. Crossing safely at a foot overbridge or FOB may involve a walk of up to a couple of kilometres.

Of course, there are other ways to cross. People have discovered that although it's illegal, it's actually possible to cross at many unfenced points along the railway line, some of which are actually not that far away from the stations themselves. The gain is the time and effort saved getting to a safe crossing, but the cost can be brutally high. A staggering 40,000 people have died and an equal number were injured trying to cross the tracks between 2002 and 2011, as revealed by a request under India's Right to Information Act. Every year, 15,000 people die on railway tracks throughout India,

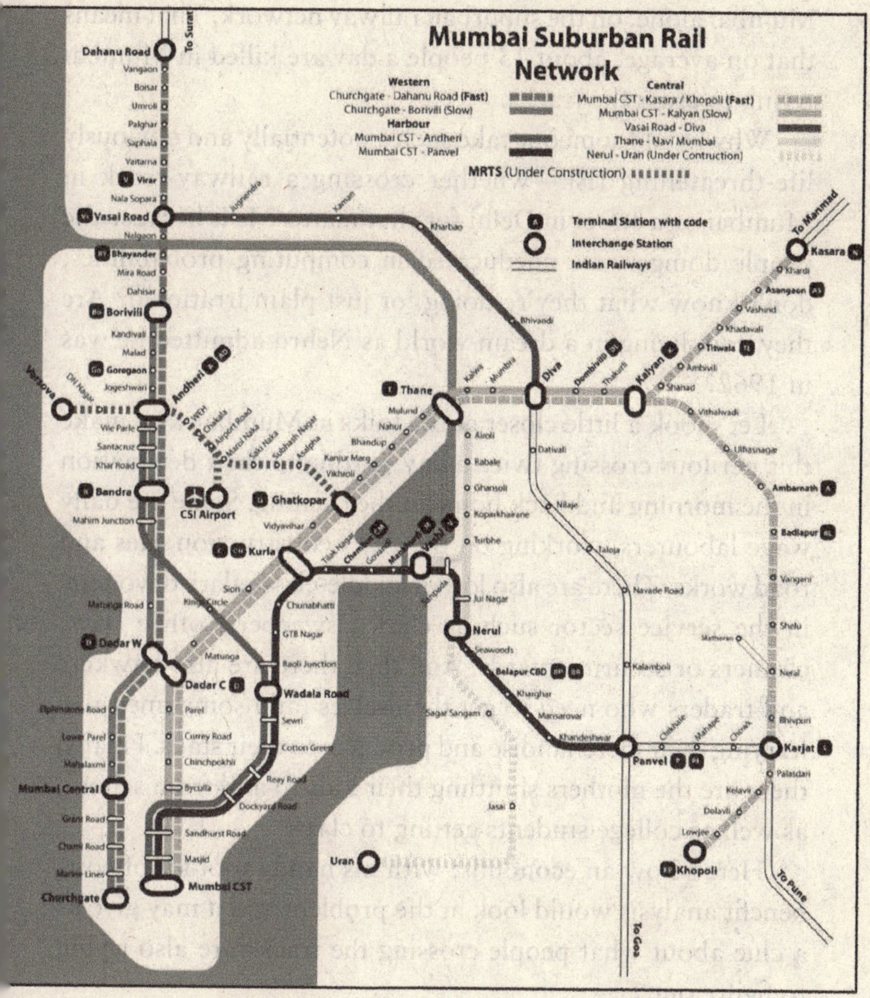

Map of Mumbai's suburban railway networks
Source: Indian Railway Catering and Tourism Corporation

of which 40 per cent, or about 6,000 deaths take place in Mumbai alone, on the suburban railway network. That means that on average, about 15 people a day are killed in Mumbai trying to cross the tracks.

Why would someone take such a potentially and obviously life-threatening risk—whether crossing a railway track in Mumbai or a street in Delhi for that matter? Is it because the people doing it are uneducated in computing probabilities, don't know what they're doing, or just plain irrational? Are they, too, living in a dream world as Nehru admitted he was in 1962?

Let's look a little closer at the folks in Mumbai who make this perilous crossing twice a day, getting to their destination in the morning and back home in the evening. Some are daily wage labourers, working on the city's construction sites and road works. There are also lower-middle-class salaried workers in the service sector such as clerks, sweepers, office boys, cleaners or security guards. And then there are also hawkers and traders who need to get themselves (and sometimes also ferrying their merchandise and produce) to their stalls. Finally, there are the mothers shuttling their kids to and from school, as well as college students getting to class.

Here's how an economist with his handy tool-kit of cost-benefit analysis would look at the problem and it may give us a clue about what people crossing the tracks are also trying to figure out.

Take Kalu, a migrant from Bihar, who earns a living as a daily wage labourer and has to commute to a construction site in south Mumbai. If he doesn't get to the site on time, he'll definitely be passed over by the foreman and won't earn money that day. Shaving even a half hour off his commute could be hugely beneficial: it might mean the difference between eating that day or going hungry. The 'cost' is uncertain: it's the likelihood of being struck by a train and being killed on the spot. The choice is clear for Kalu and tens of thousands like him: it's better to run a small risk of being killed for the certain reward of a day's earnings. By the same token, in many Indian cities, people, whether rich or poor, educated or not, will cross the road illegally and at the peril of being hit by oncoming cars because it's just too far out of your way to walk to the next traffic light or pedestrian subway. (We plead guilty to doing this on many occasions.) Presumably, they're making the same calculation.

Kalu and the many others who cross have shown us their assessment of the cost-benefit calculation: since they're crossing, they've 'revealed' that for them the benefit exceeds the cost. So why not, say, just build a bunch of FOBs and change the cost-benefit trade-off for Kalu and others like him who risk their lives every day?

If there were an FOB a short walk away, it would reduce the time cost of using one, and make someone more inclined not to take a risk of crossing unsafely. For one thing, even a wealthy city such as Mumbai has different constituencies clamouring for public funds. Resources, even if they're large by Indian standards, aren't unlimited. So if the city did decide, say, to erect an FOB every few hundred metres, that would be resources taken away from other public goods, such as schools, hospitals, roads, flyovers, and so on. But even if there were the resources to build a whole bunch of FOBs, it would be enormously disruptive to the city's economy. The railways are lifelines for the city, the financial hub of India, and even a closure of a few hours a day would lead to millions of dollars of economic loss. As a second possibility, how about just increasing the fine and hiring a whole lot more municipal workers to enforce it? Again, that bright idea is going to hit some serious resource constraints. With tens of thousands of people crossing every day, along some 60 kilometres of track, the city would have to put thousands of people on the payroll, and even then it would be a hit and miss operation, to say nothing of making us more like a police state than anyone would care for.

Might there be another way to get people to *change* their behaviour and cross where it's safe? And should we even be asking this question, if everyone crossing is behaving *rationally*?

IV

Unless you're an economist yourself, it probably doesn't come as a surprise to you that people don't always behave rationally. Conventional economists are used to thinking about a world in which everyone is fully rational, perfectly informed, and has unlimited reasoning capabilities as well as being completely self-controlled. Even if we don't believe it's literally true, this theory can be a great way to help us understand the incentives that people face and the ways they may act in many situations. Sometimes, the usual economic assumption of the rational person makes good sense. As a classic example, the textbook theories of demand and supply, or the beneficial effects of international trade, can be well explained using the conventional rational actor theory. The perfectly rational actor is, indeed, the foundation of conventional or 'neoclassical' economics. Other times, however, it can lead us seriously astray.

Cognitive psychologists Daniel Kahneman and Amos Tversky were pioneers in the study of the cognitive biases and failures that real human beings, rather than the conventional economist's textbook 'maximizer', are prone to. We're given to all sorts of systematic mistakes, whether it's being influenced by the way a choice is framed, tending to pick the 'default' option because it's easier than thinking through the alternatives, disliking losses more than we like gains ('loss aversion'), or being prone to inertia (the 'status quo bias'). Kahneman and Tversky spent decades studying these departures from rationality systematically. They carefully documented the range of cognitive biases and failures that result from our human frailties that cause us, more often than not, to behave differently from rational, selfish, calculating machines who always know what we're doing. The insights coming from their research, and of other cognitive psychologists, slowly began working their way into economics and chipping away at the façade of the always rational person. A new field—'behavioural economics'—was born, punctuated by Kahneman—a psychologist—winning the Nobel Prize in Economics back in 2002. Tversky was robbed by his early death from sharing the Nobel Prize. As it turned out, Kahneman shared the prize with Vernon Smith, who pioneered the field of 'experimental economics', which grew in tandem with behavioural economics. The two new fields together challenged the hegemony of conventional economics' assumption of the always rational person.

Can these insights help us understand an historical episode such as a war? Or why people gamble? Or cross dangerous train tracks for that matter?

Let's start by taking another look at the 1962 war, and what Nehru said in the aftermath of India's defeat:

> *We were living in an artificial atmosphere of our own creation.*

And Shashi Tharoor's assessment of Nehru's statement to Parliament in August 1961, appealing to 'wisdom and strength', he dismisses as 'complacent banalities that revealed neither wisdom nor strength'.

To us, the picture that emerges is that, in the lead-up to the war, Nehru *might*, perhaps, have succumbed to a cognitive bias, and woken up to that reality when it was already too late. From greatly underestimating the possibility of war and the resolve of the Chinese, India's humiliating defeat in the war forced him to re-evaluate his original assessment. With great candour and self-awareness, Nehru admitted that he'd been living in a dream world before the war broke out. His unrealistic perceptions before the outbreak of war, unconnected apparently to the ground reality, certainly suggest as much.

And let's not forget that India's defeat in the 1962 war isn't all about Nehru. There was certainly a role played by the controversial and flamboyant defence minister, V.K. Krishna Menon. Indeed, he took a good chunk of the blame, his position became untenable after the war, and he was forced to resign his ministerial post—even his good friend Nehru couldn't save him. By all accounts brilliantly intellectual and eccentric, Krishna Menon was also, in Tharoor's words, a 'leftist ideologue' who, among other foibles, refused to import foreign military equipment because of his belief in the doctrine of self-reliance. His leftist leanings also most likely blinded him to the Chinese threat. Krishna Menon shared with Nehru the naïvely optimistic view that China, being a fellow Asian and socialist state, would never attack India for that reason, showing an evident blind spot to Chinese nationalism that had been detected as long ago as 1950 by the shrewd and clear-eyed Vallabhai Patel. (Vallabhai Patel was, along with Nehru, one of the leaders of the Congress Party that helped India win freedom from British rule. After independence, when Nehru became prime minister, Patel became home minister, in which capacity he oversaw the absorption of the 'princely states' into independent India.)

It was a perfect storm: a prime minister, and his trusted ally, the defence minister, both turning a blind eye to the Chinese threat and at variance with the clear and present danger. *Maybe* Nehru and Krishna Menon were filtering out warning signals on the eve of war with China? *Could* they have been suffering from one or more cognitive biases and failures—an ideological stance (which you can call 'idealism' if you prefer) which made them discount the danger, laced with overconfidence about India's military capabilities—in understanding and dealing with the Chinese threat? We conjecture that the answer may be 'yes'. Perhaps it wasn't inevitable, but the particular cognitive failures we think might have been at work surely contributed to India's ill-preparedness and ultimate defeat at the hands of the Chinese.

It turns out that drastic changes in assessments that don't seem to reflect a change in objective circumstances, such as Nehru's very different views of the Chinese threat before and after the 1962 war, are a notable feature of many episodes of war. The political scientists Dominic Johnson of Edinburgh University and Dominic Tierney of Swarthmore College argue that in the months leading up to the outbreak of the First World War, political and military leaders of the great European powers were very cautious in their assessments of their enemies' strengths and capabilities when conflict was still distant. But as conflict neared, they adopted strikingly more optimistic assessments of their own relative strengths and downgraded their estimates of their enemies', although the facts on the ground hadn't changed. This change of perception, they suggest, made the outbreak of war much more likely once, as they put it metaphorically, the Rubicon had been crossed. This refers to the famous episode in 49 BCE when Julius Caesar stopped his army at the banks of the Rubicon river in northern Italy. Crossing it would, according to Roman convention, signal his intention to go to war. He did indeed cross, and the rest is history. In Johnson and Tierney's conceptual framework, politicians on the eve of the First World War switched from a 'deliberative' to an 'implemental' mindset. They argue that this triggered a number of psychological biases among the leaders of the countries involved, especially the 'overconfidence bias', a cognitive bias well-documented by psychologists such as Kahneman and Tversky.

Let's take a specific episode from the First World War. Historians Eliot Cohen and John Gooch, in their book *Military Misfortunes*, document a famous military debacle brought on by overconfidence, which was the invasion of Gallipoli led by British forces. By attacking this peninsula in the south of Turkey, the British plan was to break the stalemate on the Western Front and attack Germany through southern Europe. To make a long and messy story short, the invasion was a disaster, the British suffered a humiliating military defeat, and the Ottoman Empire then in its dying days had a final burst of glory on the battlefield. Taking a cue from Cohen and Gooch's book, Dominic Johnson in his book *Overconfidence and War: The Havoc and Glory of Positive Illusions*, argues that this failed invasion was a case of 'severe overconfidence'.

Tierney tells us that overconfidence is 'endemic, and seems to spike when leaders believe that conflict is imminent'. While he doesn't claim that his and Johnson's theory necessarily explains the 1962 war, we think it's at least suggestive of a similar pattern of behaviour by Indian leaders.

Looking at historical events such as the India–China war or the First World War is a great reminder that the world doesn't always evolve according to a rational plan and, conversely, rationality sometimes, perhaps often, deserts human beings. Even Nehru's most severe critics would never suggest that he would knowingly lead India into a military defeat. And Krishna Menon has been called arrogant, incompetent, and ineffective by many, but never a traitor. Their failures were not of sincerity in their beliefs or plans (although you can certainly question the wisdom of Indian military planning), but rather seriously underestimating the Chinese threat and failing to understand the information the Chinese were conveying through their actions and statements. And underestimating the threat from an enemy is the flip side of overconfidence in dealing with the threat that they pose. It's like someone ignoring a thousand different hints from their partner that things aren't going well in the relationship and being surprised when one day they just pack up and leave you for someone else.

Of course, we shouldn't single out Nehru, Krishna Menon, or just political or military leaders: psychological research by Kahneman, Tversky, and others tells us that there are cognitive biases and failures all humans are prone to, of which we ourselves are unaware, and can affect our perceptions and actions at a very deep level. Politicians are no more immune from these than the rest of us. The difference is that a cognitive failure from a political leader at a time of crisis can have disastrous consequences.

The overconfidence bias also helps us explain why folks are willing to buy lottery tickets or flock to casinos: overestimating your chance of success. In the case of a gamble, more precisely, it's overestimating the odds in your favour. Strictly speaking, the psychological mechanism concerns what's called 'skewness'. A lottery, like Mega Millions, has a tiny probability of giving you a huge win, and a big probability of giving you nothing. Yet, we fixate on the small chance of the big win and discount the large chance of winning nothing. This amounts, in effect, to overestimating our chance of winning. It's also why it's much more effective to hand someone a coupon which gives them a tiny chance of winning 5,000 rupees rather than giving everyone say five rupees in cash. Although economic calculation would say that five rupees in your pocket is worth more than almost no chance of winning 5,000 rupees, most people prefer the gamble. That's the psychological insight that the Delhi police had cottoned on to.

You don't have to have heard of Kahneman or Tverksy to realize that the way choices are put to us can affect our decisions, even when they shouldn't. And that couldn't possibly make sense in a world in which everyone's always rational and immune to having their decisions framed for them. Advertisers and marketing experts have known forever that the way to sell something is not just to list all of its great attributes—which is all the rational consumer would care about—but to create a positive psychological association for the would-be purchaser or just grab their attention, by ensuring that their product is placed at eye level or close to the checkout counter. And as we saw with the overconfidence bias, governments that sell lottery tickets or casinos that invite us to gamble in them have also figured out that folks aren't always totally rational but susceptible to psychological influence. And as we believe the 1962 India–China war showed us too, politicians can also succumb to overconfidence, with important consequences for all of us.

V

The early research by Kahneman, Tversky, and others documented cognitive failures mostly using test subjects in rich countries such as the US or middle income countries such as Israel. In fact, cognitive failures are at least as, if not more, important in a country like India which has many poor people. As well documented in *Poor Economics*, an award-winning book published in 2011 by Abhijit Banerjee and Esther Duflo, two economics professors at MIT, the behaviour of the poor in India and elsewhere doesn't neatly fit the pattern of rational behaviour that economists normally assume. For example, even very poor people, who barely have enough to eat, will indulge in luxury consumption such as buying TVs or spending a lot of money on festivals.

Why might this be?

As early as 2004, economics professors Marianne Bertrand at the University of Chicago, Sendhil Mullainathan at Harvard, and psychology professor Eldar Shafir at Princeton, made the case that it's the particular circumstances that the poor face which make them especially susceptible to cognitive failure. In simple terms, the poor have less 'slack' than the rest of us to make up for these deficiencies. For many of you reading this book in India, you can probably also afford to occasionally indulge in a drink or maybe even splurge by going out to a fancy restaurant or enjoying a weekend at a resort. You might regret it the next day because it's more than you wanted to spend, but it's not going to set your life on a downward spiral. At the very most, you'll just have to refrain from indulging next month or rack up some interest charges on your credit card.

But for someone very poor, like a daily wage labourer, there isn't this slack. When they indulge—and it could be as simple as having two or three drinks one evening after work—they might go hungry the next day because they've spent a day's wages. And so resisting temptation uses up a lot more mental energy for the poor than the well-to-do, because for someone very poor, temptations lurk around every corner—even a small indulgence can break the bank and has to be constantly guarded against. Plus, because they're working so hard just to survive, the poor have less time, and so fewer mental resources, to devote to thinking coolly and calmly. That again depletes cognitive resources and makes them more likely to succumb to cognitive failure, by resorting to intuition and instinct when they're just too mentally spent to reason and reflect.

The possibility of cognitive failure when we're especially challenged or stressed, of course, applies to all of us. It's normal to be cranky and to underperform after skipping a meal or not getting a proper night's sleep. And being hungry or tired tends to lead to bad judgement calls and poor decisions. The same goes for when we have extra stress in our lives—work, family, illness—all of these challenge our cognitive faculties and make us more prone to biases and failures. In a place like India, add to that the everyday stress caused by heat, humidity, noise, dust, pollution, traffic, bad roads, water and power cuts, constant bureaucracy, corruption, negotiating with your maid or watchman, worrying about exams and school admissions, and perhaps dealing with a joint family. Rich or poor, we all face these problems all the time. At least, the well-to-do can come back to the comfort of a clean and safe home and a hot meal, unwind over a glass of wine, or take an occasional vacation to recharge their mental and emotional batteries. The poor don't have any of these outlets: they're grinding it out all the time. They face challenges to their cognitive abilities in spades.

More recently, Mullainathan and Shafir, together with Anandi Mani, an economics professor at the University of Warwick, conducted field research in India, and their findings back up these ideas. They interviewed sugarcane farmers in the southern state of Tamil Nadu both before and after the harvests. Before the harvest, it's unclear how rich the crop will be and there's a great deal of uncertainty, making material (and cognitive) resources scarce. In simple terms, they simply don't know how much they're going to have when the crop does come in, and if it will be enough to pay their bills and look after themselves and their families. After the harvest, when the value of the crop is known, at least some uncertainty has been resolved and resource constraints are a little less tight than they were before. The scholars performed standard psychological tests for aptitude and ability that require people to use their reasoning abilities and not rely on potentially faulty intuition. They found that the farmers scored noticeably better after the harvest than before. In other words, their cognitive failures and biases were more pronounced when they were more constrained (and poorer) than when they were less so.

VI

Does the risky choice of crossing a busy railway line make any sense? According to the cost-benefit story, it seems to. Beyond pointing out the danger to someone, any further attempt to cajole or coerce people into changing their choices would be illiberal and paternalistic, both cardinal sins for the economist and political libertarian. But that conclusion assumes that everyone doing the crossing is a rational, calculating machine. By now, we know that might not always be true.

Suppose the folks crossing the tracks aren't always fully rational and are prone to cognitive failure? The Indian Railway's traditional approach to deter people from crossing, as in much of the world, was to put up warning signs with stick figures and lots of explanatory text. But maybe the people crossing every day were just 'filtering' out these boiler-plate warning signs and so underestimating the danger to themselves.

It's more than likely that the folks (many of whom are poor) crossing the train tracks are succumbing, without realizing it, to one or another kind of cognitive bias or failure. For example, they might be overconfident about their ability to cross safely, and so overestimate the odds in their favour. For another, they might simply be crossing out of habit, rather than thinking it through each time, a form of the status quo bias.

The pervasiveness of such biases opens up the possibility of influencing people's choice in a way that isn't blatantly paternalistic. In 2008 behavioural economist Richard Thaler and legal scholar Cass Sunstein, who were then both at the University of Chicago, published an influential and best-selling book, *Nudge*. It's been so influential, in fact, that Sunstein worked for the Obama administration in the US, where it's said he 'wielded enormous power' trying to put his theories into practice.The book is the intellectual foundation of a group in the British prime minister's office known as the Behavioural Insight Team—a name which would surely have pleased George Orwell.

Thaler and Sunstein make a compelling case for the new philosophy they call 'libertarian paternalism'. That would be an oxymoron for a conventional economist: either you're a libertarian, who believes in unfettered individual choice, or you're a paternalist, who believes that someone (usually the state) knows better and should guide or even force people to do what's best for themselves.

Or maybe not.

As we've already seen, how choices are framed for an individual can make a huge difference on what they end up picking. A rational, calculating person wouldn't be affected by how a choice is framed, but real people, with all of their built-in cognitive limitations, certainly could be. If we can 'nudge' people into making a better choice, Thaler and Sunstein suggest, not by coercing them but rather by presenting the choice in a different way, what's wrong with that? And the people who do the nudging don't have to be the government, they could be anyone who has an influence on the way your choice is framed: in their words, a 'choice architect'. As we've seen that the poor are especially susceptible to cognitive failures because of their difficult circumstances, the case for thoughtful 'nudges' is, if anything, stronger in a place like India than in the Western context that Thaler and Sunstein originally had in mind.

Around the same time that Thaler and Sunstein's book came out, a group of young consultants with a background in advertising and a passion for the science of human behaviour came together to start a consulting firm called FinalMile. Calling themselves 'thought architects', they decided to apply the lessons from behavioural economics and cognitive neuroscience to their consulting assignments. As it turns out, they were to develop an approach to tackling the problem of the deaths on Mumbai's train tracks that Thaler and Sunstein would approve of.

Biju Dominic, a former ad man and a co-founder of FinalMile, learned about the daily tragedies on the Mumbai rail system while teaching a class at the railway's staff college. He felt that what was needed was a series of interventions or 'nudges' which would get people, who were obviously filtering out the generic warning signs, to realize the danger of crossing and make them think twice before doing it. The railway authorities were impressed with his approach and he took it upon himself and FinalMile to work on this pro bono. As Ram Prasad, a member of the team, put it: 'We can make money selling soap, but then we can use some of that money we earn to do some good somewhere else.'

Their first step was to collect and then scour the reams of data on fatalities that are kept at all of the railway stations throughout the city. First, they had to parse the data between those who fell from overcrowded moving trains—another frequent occurrence in Mumbai—and those who had fallen on the tracks and been hit by a moving train. That drew their attention to the Wadala station on the Harbour Line of the Central Railway. It had seen the biggest spike in knock-over deaths in 2009, jumping from 17 in the first half of the year to 23 in the second half. Plus it was one of a group of eight of the most notoriously dangerous stations, accounting for about two-thirds of total fatalities in the entire railway system of Mumbai.

Wadala station would become their 'live experiment'. The team carefully observed the pattern of crossings over a period of many weeks. The first thing they noticed was that no one was crossing at the station but rather in between Wadala and the neighbouring stations in either direction. Many of those crossing were from a slum which was adjacent to one side of the station. They also deduced that the fatalities occurred at points where people were seldom crossing. Where crossings were frequent, no one had been killed. Part of the reason is that when lots of people are crossing and someone sees an oncoming train they shout '*gaadi!*' ('train!') to warn everyone else nearby. They also noticed that children were most adept at crossing the tracks. The statistics bear this out: 85 per cent of those killed crossing the tracks were adult males. Of course, this may also reflect the fact that it's mostly men who're crossing.

People who are used to crossing the tracks, often from the time they are kids, tend to underestimate the danger to their lives. This is a classic example of the 'overconfidence bias' we've already seen in so many different contexts. This could also help explain that other mystery, which is why so many people dangle from the sides of overcrowded trains, when they're clearly ignoring or underestimating the odds of being hit by a pole or falling off, which are also frequent occurrences in India.

But FinalMile's remit was to try and lessen the unsafe crossings. They designed three interventions, or 'nudges' in the language of Thaler and Sunstein, to try to make would-be crossers aware of the risks they were taking by crossing, but—if they decided to cross anyway—to increase their chances of making it alive. First, they painted alternate sets of railway ties (that's the series of metal beams that connect the two ends of a track) a bright yellow. This was to help compensate for the psychological fact that people tend to underestimate the speed of large moving objects. With alternate sets of ties painted yellow, someone would be better able to gauge the speed of an oncoming train as it passed from the painted to the unpainted ties. If you've taken a high-speed train, you know how this works: looking out of the window at a bare landscape, you have no idea how fast you're going, until another train whizzes by at high speed on the opposite track.

Second, they convinced the railway authorities to have the train drivers switch from a single long warning whistle to two short staccato bursts. This was based on neurological research, which showed that the human brain is more receptive to sound when it's separated by silence. Classical music lovers intuitively understand this: a lone cymbal crash is way more arresting if it comes after a moment of silence than in the middle of an already loud passage of music.

Third, and most strikingly, they ditched the stick figures and fine print warnings not to cross with a graphic panel in three parts of the wide-eyed horror of a real human being about to be crushed by an oncoming train. The picture depicts the actual poster at a railway station in Mumbai. They hired an actor to make it as realistic as possible. The purpose of this was to get away from the bland and generic warning someone's conscious mind would filter out and appeal to the sensation of fear in the subconscious mind. Viewers of horror movies will know exactly how this works.

All three of these nudges were rolled out at the beginning of 2010 and kept in place for the whole year. The results were dramatic. In the first half of 2010, the number of deaths dropped to nine, and in the second half there was only one fatality. That's a drop of a whopping 75 per cent from the

FinalMile poster intended to deter people from crossing the railway tracks in Mumbai
Source: FinalMile

previous year. The beneficiaries won't show up in any statistics: they're the people who saw the sign and decided not to cross, or were able to make it across because of the painted ties or staccato warning whistles. Sometimes, it's the numbers that don't appear that tell the real story.

The experiment was deemed a success by the railway authorities, and it's now gradually being rolled out throughout the entire Mumbai rail network. At the time we spoke to the folks at FinalMile in February 2012, the three interventions were being implemented by the railway itself at Mulund, Vikhroli, and Ghatkopar stations.

The idea of using psychologically attuned nudges seems to be catching on with police forces all over India. In October 2010, the police in Chennai put up gruesome billboard hoardings of people with smashed up skulls and other such horrific pictures to try to get motorcyclists to wear helmets. And in January 2012, the police in Navi Mumbai, a suburb of Mumbai on the mainland of Maharashtra, experimented with putting up two 'live' exhibits instead of the usual warning signs. They were a car and a motorbike wrecked in actual road accidents nearby. At the time of writing in 2012, it was too early to tell if these initiatives were effective in reducing accidents and fatalities. Then there is the added question of whether wearing helmets will in fact reduce accidents and fatalities. We'll look into this question in a future chapter. While still in their infancy, at the very least, like the Delhi police's innovative lottery scheme, they represent creative approaches to tackling seemingly intractable problems, by tapping into the insights of the behavioural sciences—or just plain common sense. When tested and true methods aren't working, no matter how sound the theory behind them, you've got to try to do something different.

The reality of pervasive cognitive biases and failures—especially for the poor and those in greatest distress—coupled with the possibility it creates for choice architects to influence people's behaviour, makes for great opportunities: which can be exploited for good or for ill. It gives us a whole new lens through which we can look at public policy in India and other countries: and not just for the government, but for anyone in a position to deliver one or more nudges, which push people in one direction or another. Whether it's our political leaders or a day labourer crossing the train tracks, we're all prone to make mistakes. We might aspire to the wisdom of the gods, but, when all is said and done, we're only human.

3

What If . . .?

I

India's roads can be a dangerous, even a deadly, place to be. In 2011, according to government statistics, India recorded 142,485 road fatalities—one of the highest in the world. This is one statistic where nobody likes to be the world leader. To put that in perspective, someone is killed on the road in India about every 3.7 minutes. And the number of people injured during the same period was a staggering 511,394, or one person injured on the road almost every minute. In fact, every year since 2007, more than half a million people have been injured, and more than 100,000 killed, every year due to road accidents. As we write this, we just witnessed a road accident looking out of our window in Mumbai, although fortunately, not a fatal one.

If it's any consolation, on a per capita basis, although not in absolute numbers, things aren't as bad in India as they are in some other countries. Again, according to government statistics, in 2009, there were 10.83 fatalities per 100,000 of population. That puts India about in the middle of the pack when it comes to emerging countries, slightly worse, say, than Indonesia (8.69), but much better than, say, Malaysia (24.56). But India is still doing much worse than Western countries when it comes to road fatalities. The comparable statistic for most Western countries is in the range of five to seven deaths per 100,000, significantly better than India. The US, as in many other areas, is an exception in the Western world. Its road accident death rate per 100,000 is 11.01, slightly worse than India. But it could also be, of course, that reporting is better in the US than in India, so this comparison should be taken with a pinch of salt.

As early as 1994, hoping to curb road fatalities, the central government imposed a regulation that required car-makers to equip the front seats of all new cars with lap and shoulder belts, although motorcycles and three-wheelers with small engines were exempted. Taking the next step, in March 1999, the government further mandated the use of seatbelts by passengers in the front compartment. Since traffic laws are a state jurisdiction under India's federal constitution, each state decides how to interpret and enforce the seatbelt law. In Delhi, the nation's capital, for example, the traffic police began enforcing the seatbelt rule in February 2002. Being caught without a seatbelt in the front cabin would lead to a fine of 100 rupees for the first infraction and 300 rupees for every subsequent violation.

Seatbelt laws and government regulations to make cars safer to drive first appeared in a big way in the US. In 1968, the federal government imposed safety requirements on all new cars sold in the US. Among other things, there now had to be seatbelts for all occupants, a steering column which absorbed the energy of an impact, a windshield which would resist breakage in an accident, a dual breaking system, and a padded instrument panel. Most people had assumed that safer cars would automatically lead to greater road safety. The science seemed to back them up. A wide range of technological studies by researchers working for the US government, as well as by scholars in universities and the private sector, established that highway deaths in the US would have been anywhere from 10–25 per cent higher—about 20 per cent, averaging across these studies—without the new safety equipment. These studies typically compared the survival rate of someone in a road accident, with and without safety equipment such as seatbelts, by using crash test dummies. What's more, accident statistics showed a steady decline through the 1960s and even beyond. That seemed to suggest that the new equipment was, in fact, saving lives.

End of story, right?

In 1975, Sam Peltzman, an economics professor at the University of Chicago Business School, wanted to investigate these claims through economics, not taking on faith what the techies were saying or the glowing reports coming out of the US government safety regulator every year. Peltzman was thinking like an economist, not an engineer, and realized that to really know if safety equipment saves lives you need to compare the *actual* safety record after they were mandated with what *would* have happened *if* they hadn't been introduced. In other words, you need to perform a 'counterfactual' exercise. Simply put, this means you have to compare the situation we're in right now—our real world—with a sensible and meaningful alternative scenario—the counterfactual.

To see how it works, take a different example. Let's say an economist at India's Planning Commission (the Indian government's in-house think tank) in New Delhi is wondering if a 10 per cent increase in kerosene prices would be a good thing for the government to do. Could they just look at the marketplace today to answer the question? No. They'd have to figure out what would happen to the demand and supply of kerosene if the price were increased and what kind of knock-on effects this would have on the rest of the economy. It would in effect be a counterfactual experiment in which the planners compare our actual world with an alternate fictional world (but one they might want to transport us to) in which the price of kerosene is 10 per cent higher.

As another example, suppose the Reserve Bank of India (India's central bank) was worried about the inflation rate becoming too high and wanted to consider the impact of tightening the money supply by 10 per cent. They, too, would run a simulated mathematical model—this time, a macroeconomic model, not just demand and supply—and compare the inflation rate that this tighter monetary policy would give in the simulated model as compared to the actual inflation rate in the real world. Again—this is a type of counterfactual exercise. Macroeconomic models as used by central banks are typically large mathematical models that try to capture the effects of changes in monetary policy (interest rates, the money supply, etc.) on all sectors of the economy put together and their interactions. A demand and supply model, typical in microeconomics, normally looks instead at one sector of the economy.

Now doing a counterfactual experiment using demand and supply or a macroeconomic model doesn't sound too hard. All you have to have is a semi-decent statistical or mathematical model and crunch some numbers. That's what the good folks at the plan panel, the central bank, and other government agencies, to say nothing of private sector consulting firms, do to earn their living. If you have good quantitative skills, you might actually make a lot of money working for an investment bank or consulting firm, which, in effect, perform counterfactual experiments for their clients all the time.

What made Peltzman's counterfactual exercise different and unique was that, in the tradition of the 'Chicago School' of economics, he was applying it to a terrain—the life-saving effects of automobile safety equipment—which until then had been thought to be within the domain of science and technology, not economics. Would Peltzman's economic approach make a difference to the results?

What he found was truly amazing: the claims made about fewer deaths thanks to the new safety equipment didn't hold up to scrutiny. The technology gurus and the government regulators were wrong. The greater safety generated by safer cars was 'offset' by the fact that drivers, who now felt safer, took greater risks than before. These two effects pulled in opposite directions: safer cars led to greater safety, other things equal; but rasher driving led to reduced safety, other things equal.

With unsafe cars, people who are tempted to drive rashly

are held in check by the fact that, if they make a mistake, they could get into a crash and wind up seriously injured or dead. With safer cars, these same people now have a lessened incentive to drive safely, since the 'price' of rash driving is now lower: you could get into an accident, but chances are you'll be saved by your seatbelt or other safety features. Another way of saying this is that, before safety regulations made cars safer, drivers 'purchased' their own safety plan, so to speak, by driving more prudently and taking fewer risks.

Incredibly, Peltzman found that the negative effect on overall safety of drivers' responses to the increased safety of their vehicles *completely* offset the presumed increase in safety from the new equipment: in other words, when the human factor was taken into account, there was no overall improvement in safety thanks to the new equipment! Peltzman's intuition proved correct: real people don't behave like crash test dummies. Assuming that they do, as in technology-based studies, can give us very misleading results. The life-saving gains of 10–25 per cent, promised by technology, were completely offset by the human response, and these two things just cancelled out.

Of course, in theory, offsetting could be less than 100 per cent if, for example, people drove only slightly more rashly because they felt safer, or conceivably even more than 100 per cent, if safer cars turn every driver into a Formula 1 racer. In the latter case, safety equipment would actually increase, not decrease, the accident fatality rate. It was just one of those quirky flukes that Peltzman found exactly 100 per cent offsetting: the new equipment had no beneficial effect at all, as it was totally and exactly undone by people driving more rashly and getting into more accidents. Quirky it might be, but the cottage industry of research that has followed in the wake of Peltzman's original path-breaking study has found some version or the other of his offsetting effect in action when new legislation or safety equipment is introduced ostensibly to make driving safer. For example, a 2004 study investigated the effects of automobile insurance, laws that made such insurance compulsory, and so called 'no fault' liability laws, again using US data. They found that automobile insurance actually led to an increased number of traffic fatalities. Likewise, the reduced accident liability caused by no fault liability laws also increased traffic fatalities in this case by about 6 per cent.

Could the offsetting effect hold lessons for traffic safety in India?

At the Indian Institute of Technology in Delhi, Dinesh Mohan, a professor who studies road safety, tried to evaluate how effective the seatbelt laws have been in reducing traffic fatalities in Delhi. In a scholarly study published in 2010, he and a team of researchers collected, collated and analysed statistics on seatbelt use and road accidents in Delhi. His research team went out into the streets to monitor the use of seatbelts both before and after the mandatory seatbelt law came into force in 2002. First off, the seatbelt law did get people to begin wearing seatbelts. In 2001, before the law, only 12 per cent of the people monitored actually used their seatbelts, and this jumped to 70 per cent after the law came into force the following year. The use of seatbelts by passengers in the front cabin has averaged over 70 per cent for the years since 2002. (Recall that the seatbelt law only applies to front seat and not rear seat passengers. Use of seatbelts by rear-seat passengers is almost non-existent in India, as the study also confirms.) This is even though, on average according to the study, only about 2–3 per cent of drivers in a given month who aren't wearing their seatbelts are actually stopped and fined by the police.

Data on road traffic fatalities in Delhi paint an intriguing picture. Starting from about five per 100,000 in the early 1970s, which as we noted earlier is still about the norm in developed countries of the West, this rate kept steadily rising and peaked at almost 25 by the mid-1990s. But then, fatalities began to decline after that and have been dropping more or less steadily since then, to just over 11 per 100,000 in 2008, about 34 per cent lower than the peak which was hit in 1997.

So what explains this pattern of fatalities first rising and then falling off? The earlier period represents the growth of automobile ownership in India, which took off especially after the economic liberalization of 1991. From having a choice between two makes of cars for many decades after independence, and long wait lists to even buy a car, motorists now had many more options and cars were readily available as was the financing to help purchase them. The explosive growth in car use in Delhi over the 1990s helps explain the increase in fatalities over that period. But the construction of roads, bridges, flyovers, etc. didn't keep pace with the growth in the number of vehicles, so the drop-off in the fatality rate after 1997 can best be explained by the increase in traffic congestion. In more congested traffic, as we all know, drivers have no choice but to go slow, and are often in bumper to bumper traffic, so you would expect fewer fatal accidents to occur. And this, of course, isn't unique to Delhi but applies to other big Indian cities as well, as we can painfully attest when it sometimes takes us half an hour to go a kilometre or so in our neighbourhood in Mumbai.

Let's take a look at the fatality rate for drivers and front seat passengers of cars in Delhi, the people whom the seatbelt law is presumably intended to protect. Did it actually work as planned? The fatality rate for car occupants in 2001 was 6.9 per 100,000 cars. Note that the fatality rate for car occupants will, by definition, be less than the total fatality rates we talked about earlier, because as we shall see many of the people fatally injured in road accidents are not themselves occupants of cars. In the next four years, when the seatbelt law was enforced, this fatality rate dropped off marginally, to 6.7 in 2002 and then went back up to 7.1 in 2003. Since then it's dropped off to a little below 6. So did the seatbelt law save lives?

Crunching the numbers, Mohan concludes that the seatbelt law may have saved at most 11 to 15 (!) lives per year in Delhi out of almost 2,000 fatalities of drivers or front seat passengers. That's less than 1 per cent of the total. And even this tiny number is based on the optimistic assumption that seatbelt use by the occupants of a car would be expected to save an estimated 45–60 per cent of the lives in a given car—which in turn comes from an estimate by the Centers for Disease Control in the US, in other words, a medical, not an economic study. To show how tiny the magnitudes are, even assuming that everyone wore a seatbelt, and that they saved 45–65 per cent of the lives involved, the reduction in fatalities would be less than 2 per cent.

How can this number be so low? At a superficial level, the answer is easy: the fatality rate for drivers and front seat passengers didn't drop much after the seatbelt law came in, so it can't be responsible for having saved very many lives. But a deeper look tells us the reason why so few lives would be saved by seatbelt use, as Peltzman himself noticed in his study: most of the victims of road accidents aren't drivers, or even passengers, so seatbelt use isn't going to help them. In the case of Delhi, Mohan collected fatality data from the city police for the five-year period from 2001 to 2005. His analysis of this data shows that 47 per cent, or almost half of the victims of road accidents are pedestrians. A further 10 per cent are bicyclists and 3 per cent of the rest are in other forms of non-motorized transport such as hand-pulled carts and bullock carts. All told, 61 per cent of fatalities are among those who aren't in a motor vehicle. Of those who are, a big chunk, about 26 per cent, or more than a quarter of total fatalities, are on motorized two-wheelers such as motorcycles and scooters. In fact, victims of road fatalities who're in passenger cars account for a tiny 3 per cent of the total number of deaths. So it stands to reason that reduced fatalities for this group due to seatbelt use will at best represent a small number.

What's more, offsetting seems to be at work in a big way. Drivers of private passenger cars know that their chance of being killed is very small should they get into an accident. This is why so many drivers, either of taxis or car hire services, defeat the purpose of the seatbelt by not fastening it snugly, except perhaps when they're passing a cop. We've seen many drivers in Delhi and Mumbai use something like a laundry clip to ensure that the seatbelt doesn't fasten snugly over their shoulders and lap: a low-tech but effective form of offsetting behaviour! Therefore, whether wearing a seatbelt or not, they've got no particular personal incentive to drive more safely. The many pedestrians who're killed represent, in a sense, a tragic measure of the offsetting effect.

One suggestion for reducing fatalities for drivers or passengers of cars further might be to mandate airbags as is the case in many Western countries. The argument would be that airbags are more effective at saving lives than seatbelt use alone because they work passively, without requiring the driver or the passenger to do anything. It's theoretically a possibility that airbags could reduce fatalities—except that we have a sneaking suspicion that yet another 'offsetting' effect would kick in. Drivers who felt safer because of airbags might drive more rashly, and so a technological fix that ignores the human dimension probably won't solve the problem.

There's a pattern here. Here's an example from a totally different arena: professional sports. There's some evidence that sports which use protective gear (such as hockey and American football) see more violence on the field and hence more, rather than fewer, injuries. The reason is analogous: athletes who feel safer because of fancy protective gear are likely to be more aggressive and take more risks, thus offsetting the effects of the safety gear.

Whether it's seatbelts or hockey masks, Sam Peltzman had hit on something really important: that human behaviour can offset the effect of a well-intentioned government intervention, and end up not improving things or even making them worse. It took an economist's lens, which looks at a real world counterfactual and not a hypothetical world inhabited by test dummies, to come to this insight. Indeed, it's often called the 'Peltzman effect', and it shows up in all kinds of places where you might have least expected it.

Around the same time Sam Peltzman was doing his research in Chicago, a world away, leaders in India and China, as in many developing countries, were worried about rapid population growth and wanted to bring down fertility rates. China instituted the famous, many would call it notorious, 'one child policy'. India didn't have anything quite as draconian, yet during the Emergency—a brief period when it looked like India would slip from democracy into authoritarianism—Sanjay Gandhi, the favoured son and presumptive heir to the country's (authoritarian, if not dictatorial) prime minister, Indira Gandhi—enforced a mass sterilization campaign that scarred many rural families. Later, the government made ready access to abortion available, in the hopes that this would lead to reduced fertility. Added to that, ultra-sound scanners, which became widespread and affordable to the middle class, would allow prospective parents to screen out babies with, say, genetic defects. What no one foresaw was that in son-obsessed India and China, and elsewhere, the real result was sex-selective abortion: female foetuses being aborted by parents who wanted to have a small family and now had a way—short of infanticide—to select a boy. The millions of unborn women in the world might represent offsetting behaviour by their parents—that's why they don't exist.

II

The *Hindustan Times*, one of India's leading newspapers, and CNN-IBN, the Indian partner of the CNN network, conducted an opinion poll in late 2011 on the 'state of democracy in India'. The results are startling in the world's largest democracy. Fully a third of those surveyed agreed that the country needs a 'strong leader who does not have to bother about contesting elections'. Almost 23 per cent preferred 'experts and professionals not answerable to political leaders', while almost 10 per cent thought that politicians should rely on such people for 'governing key sectors'. More than 15 per cent would even go for the army over elected politicians. All in all, that leaves less than 20 per cent of people surveyed who actually want elected politicians to lead the country.

And if you think that poll was a fluke, think again. In 2008, a group of researchers from the UK and India conducted a large survey on attitudes to democracy throughout South Asia. The survey included almost 20,000 respondents and covered the period from August 2004 to February 2005. The Indian numbers were better than those in neighbouring countries, but still make for sobering reading. Fully 21 per cent of respondents in India said it didn't matter whether the government was democratic or not. Only 41 per cent of respondents in India classified themselves as 'strong democrats' who unequivocally preferred democracy to all other systems. That means that fully 58 per cent of Indian respondents were either 'weak democrats' (who generally preferred democracy but were open to elements of authoritarian rule) or 'non-democrats' (who always preferred authoritarian rule such as dictatorship or army rule or didn't care either way).

Pundits and scholars love to contrast India's messy democracy with China's authoritarian but efficient administration, and many impute the difference in the two countries' economic performance to the difference in their political systems. It's almost commonplace in some academic and policy circles to assume that this is why China has outperformed India for the last several decades. This view also finds favour, not surprisingly, with autocratic politicians. Lee Kwan Yew, founding prime minister of Singapore, famously supported the Chinese crackdown on protestors at Tiananmen Square in 1989, arguing that's what saved the country from an 'implosion'. On another occasion, he said: 'I believe what a country needs to develop is discipline more than democracy. The exuberance of democracy leads to indiscipline and disorderly conduct which are inimical to development.' Echoing this theme, on a visit to India in 2011, Malaysia's former autocratic leader, Mahathir Mohammed, said India needed 'less democracy' if it wanted to achieve Chinese-style double-digit growth rates.

It's not hard to see why people polled are frustrated. India's political system, for all of its democratic virtues, has produced an environment rife with corruption, excessive bureaucracy, poor infrastructure, a creaky criminal justice system, and an economy that has failed to harness the potential of hundreds of millions of its citizens. The surveys we cite give us a more scientific basis for believing that many middle-class urban Indians (the group polled) hold the same views as critics of democracy such as Lee or Mahathir, or at any rate claim they do (after all, when push comes to shove, how many people would give up democratic freedoms that they actually enjoy?). But perhaps it's not surprising, given that turnout rates in elections are among the lowest for this same group. It seems that the urban middle class, or at least a significant chunk of it, is disengaged from the political process and animated more by protest movements such as the anti-corruption crusade led by social activist Anna Hazare and his 'team' that galvanized many people in 2011 in cities across India. China, which locks up enemies of the regime and censors the internet, has pulled hundreds of millions more out of poverty than India's shambolic democracy.

When you look back on the history of the twentieth century—in fact through human history—you notice periods of very high economic growth are associated with autocratic, not democratic, regimes. Just think of Chile under the dictatorship of Augusto Pinochet or the 'miracle' economies of East Asia—Hong Kong, Singapore, South Korea, and Taiwan. Starting in the 1960s these four economies went from being poor to being rich in just over a generation. The first one was a British colony, the second an oligarchy, and the latter two essentially one-party states. It's true that Chile, Taiwan, and South Korea democratized—but that was *after* they'd experienced a generation of rapid growth, not before. (Hong Kong was the only one of the four Asian 'tigers' that couldn't democratize, for the good reason that it went from being a British colony to being ruled by mainland China during the handover of power in 1997.)

If we look even further back at history, all of the rich countries of the West achieved their rapid growth and economic development when they weren't democracies. Just think of Britain during the Industrial Revolution. While it's true that Britain was a parliamentary democracy it came with one catch, the fact that most people couldn't vote. Franchise restrictions based on property ownership meant that the poor and lower middle classes were prevented from voting. Britain was really an oligarchy, not a democracy, and so too was the US and every other Western country that industrialized and got rich. The US, for example, only legally enfranchised African-Americans after their emancipation from slavery, but this was 'offset' by franchise restrictions that meant most southern blacks couldn't participate in the political process until the civil rights movement of the 1960s. And let's not forget that women didn't get the vote in all of these Western countries till very late—well into the twentieth century in many cases. For much of their early 'democratic' history, then, half or more of the population was automatically disenfranchised in today's Western democracies.

India is unique, having emerged as a postcolonial state with universal franchise. India was a true democracy from the moment of its birth as an independent nation. That certainly wasn't what the former colonial ruler, and for that matter many elite Indians, wanted at independence. In the dying days of

British India, the Constituent Assembly had been elected (and that, too, indirectly by the provincial assemblies) under a very limited franchise, and represented the interests of at most 5 per cent or 10 per cent of Indians at the top of the socio-economic pyramid. As things turned out, Nehru and the other founders of the Indian republic opted for full democracy, putting their faith in the hundreds of millions of people who'd never tasted freedom before.

China took a different path. In 1949, after the revolution which overthrew the Nationalists, the Communist Party took absolute control over political power in the country, and hasn't relinquished it since. Apart from a few well-known dissidents, as far as we can tell given how opaque Chinese society is to outsiders, most Chinese people seem to like their system just fine, at least for now, or at least don't dislike it so much to have risen up en masse to topple the Communist regime. And regardless of what they may think of the Communist Party's monopoly on political power, many clearly appreciate the fact that it's delivered so many of them out of poverty and created opportunities for the entrepreneurial urban middle classes to strike it rich. In fact, in contemporary China, you could argue it's capitalism—or 'socialism with Chinese characteristics', as Deng Xiaoping, the Chinese leader who opened up the economy in 1979, famously called it—that's the glue that holds the country together.

To its supporters such as Singapore's Lee, and even to its grudging detractors, the Chinese system seems to represent something like a 'benevolent dictatorship' that has catapulted the country into contention with the West as a legitimate candidate to be the twenty-first century's new 'great power'. Even the most enthusiastic India boosters will concede that we're lagging far behind China in this aspiration. After India's defeat at the hands of China in the 1962 war, even Indira Gandhi had her doubts about India's political system. In 1963, she had written to a friend complaining of 'the price we pay for democracy [which] not only throws up the mediocre person but gives strength to the most vocal howsoever they may lack knowledge and understanding'. And at least if you judge by the survey results we cited earlier, urban middle-class Indians seem to agree with Mrs Gandhi's assessment and think that India ought to trade some of its messy democracy for more authoritarian control if that would buy more rapid economic development. Of course, we're not suggesting that all of India's problems, or even many of them, are traceable to democracy specifically, but rather ills such as corruption and cronyism that can occur in any political system. And poor Indians vote in record numbers election after election. Still, the survey results do capture some of the malaise with India's brand of democracy and raise the question whether a more controlled, authoritarian system could do better.

But what if we'd conducted another poll, and posed the same question in a different way. Suppose we'd asked: Would India have been better off emulating Zimbabwe, where one strong leader has ruled the country for decades? We think the answers would have been different, since, unlike China, contemporary Zimbabwe evokes quite different sentiments for those of us watching it from the outside. Zimbabwe, after a promising start when it freed itself from white minority rule in 1979, has slid into stagnation and hyperinflation under the wayward and oppressive rule of Robert Mugabe, and is the very opposite of the Chinese success story. What was once a bread basket has become a basket case.

If you had one answer when the comparison was China, and a different one when it was Zimbabwe, you've just fallen victim to what economists, borrowing from statisticians, call the 'selection bias'. If we ask whether authoritarian regimes deliver more growth than democracies, and then look only at countries that we know—after the fact—have been successful, chances are we'll bias ourselves toward a positive judgement merely because of what we chose to look at. If we'd looked instead at Zimbabwe, Haiti, or any number of failed or failing authoritarian states around the world, we'd more than likely have concluded that India's slow-but-steady democracy has done well.

In fact, India too, had its flirtation with authoritarian rule—the Emergency that we already mentioned in the context of Sanjay Gandhi's enforced sterilization scheme. For almost two years, from June 26, 1975 to March 21, 1977, Prime Minister Indira Gandhi suspended civil liberties, locked up opposition leaders, muzzled the press, and ruled the country virtually by decree. She even got a pliant Parliament to amend the constitution to legalize her 'judicial coup' after the fact, although these changes were later reversed. For better or worse, India's experience of Chinese-style authoritarianism was too short to conclude one way or the other whether its continuation for another decade or more would have been good for the country's economic development. We can speculate, but there simply isn't the data to take a definite call. Shashi Tharoor, writer and a politician in today's descendent of Indira Gandhi's Congress Party, sifts the arguments and evidence. His conclusion is forthright: 'The abuses of the Emergency far outweighed what little good it did.'

What the data *do* show is that autocracies have many more highs and lows than democracies: they tend to be spectacularly successful or unmitigated disasters. Democracies generally are found somewhere in the middle. India, for example, hasn't yet achieved Chinese-style double-digit growth rates, but nor has it ever had negative double-digit growth as in Zimbabwe. So when we look around for countries with high, rather than low or negative, growth rates, our attention is naturally attracted by the autocratic success stories like China. If we'd looked instead for countries with very low or even negative growth rates, our attention would have been drawn to the disasters like Zimbabwe.

Selection bias is a statistical problem. But it has psychological roots.

William Easterly, an economics professor at New York University, isn't afraid to challenge the conventional wisdom. After a long and distinguished career as an economist at the World Bank, where he rose up the ladder in the research department by playing by the rules, he turned 'rogue' the moment he became a free agent and has published books with provocative titles like *The Elusive Quest for Growth* and *The White Man's Burden*. In a more recent study, he's argued that it's the coming together of a series of cognitive biases—of the sort we've seen in a previous chapter in the work of Daniel Kahneman and Amos Tversky—that could explain why scholars and pundits (and maybe even the kind of people who show up in surveys) end up believing in benevolent dictatorship, even when the facts don't support them.

The first such bias is 'reversing conditional probabilities'. Here's an example. The historical data on growth over time in many different countries that Easterly has analysed show that *if* you're a fast-growing economy then there's a 90 per cent chance that you're an autocracy. This makes autocracy look pretty attractive. The problem is that you should be asking the reverse question: *if* you're an autocracy, what's the chance that you'll be a growth success? The answer to that question is an underwhelming 10 per cent.

The second bias is the 'availability heuristic'. This refers to the fact that human beings tend to attach too high a probability to an event that's very vivid in our minds. A classic example is natural disasters like earthquakes and tornadoes. Because they're splashed all over the news on the rare occasions they do occur, people always think they're far more likely than they really are. Compiling data from news stories in the *New York Times* from 1960 to 2008, Easterly shows that successful autocracies are heavily over-reported compared to failed autocracies. Compared to a little under 6,000 stories on failed autocracies and about 15,000 on those in the middle, there were a staggering number of stories—more than 40,000—on autocratic successes. So if China has been on your mind rather than Zimbabwe you're not entirely to blame.

The third bias is 'leadership attribution bias'. This means that experimental subjects tend to attribute too much credit for a given outcome to individual personalities rather than broader causes and motivations. This was something noted long ago by Leo Tolstoy in *War and Peace*. The last section of the novel is really a long philosophical essay on understanding history and dispelling the myth that flamboyant individuals like Napoleon and the Russian Czar could have had as decisive an impact on the Franco-Russian war as people thought. In the case of autocratic success stories this bias would impute too much wisdom and foresight, say to the Chinese leadership, while downplaying the role that luck and circumstance may have played. And of course in democracies such as India or the US we're used to much of the credit or blame for election outcomes being pinned to political leaders when too many other factors are at play to assign leaders such a pivotal role—this in itself represents a version of the bias.

The fourth bias goes under the colourful name the 'hot hand fallacy'. This is one that every sports fan will know and has probably committed more than a few times. The name comes from the false perception that a basketball player who has just sunk a string of baskets is more likely to sink the next one too, than his average level of skill would predict. In fact, this is false: you're no more likely to sink a basket after making the last three or four than on your first shot. In the benevolent autocrat story, we see two or three decades of rapid growth in again, say China, and we're likely to believe that this high growth will continue into the indefinite future. Indeed, while there are dissenters, most accounts of China's success story assume without much argument that the high growth will last forever.

The fifth and last bias is known as the 'law of small numbers'. A fundamental principle of statistics is that you need a large number of observations to make any valid inferences about a random event: that's the 'law of large numbers'. The human mind works differently. We tend to draw conclusions too quickly from small samples in a way that isn't statistically warranted but is psychologically hard to resist. For example, suppose you toss a coin four times and it comes up heads each time. Many of us might be tempted to conclude that it's a 'rigged' coin. In fact, a perfectly fair coin which has even odds of heads or tails will give you a string of four heads or four tails with a probability of 6.25 per cent—low, but hardly impossible. You'd need to toss the coin at least ten times to make any kind of statistically valid judgement. If you get ten heads or ten tails in a row, for example, the odds of that are less than one-tenth of one per cent, and now you'd be on good grounds to conclude that it's not a fair coin.

Likewise, as Easterly points out, it's common to declare a country a 'growth miracle' after only a few years of rapid growth. For example, Chile under Pinochet was declared a growth miracle at two different times: the first being 1977–81 and the second being 1984–89. The problem is that there was a financial crisis and crash in between both those episodes of high growth. If you looked at the whole period of 1977–89, you wouldn't have called it a miracle.

Easterly's research suggests we might want to reserve judgement on whether India or any other country would have done better economically if it were more authoritarian than democratic.

III

It's not just social scientists, then, who explore different facets of the counterfactual.

In our personal lives, we ask counterfactual questions all the time. Serious or silly, we all wonder what might have happened if we'd taken a different path, whether it's our career, our relationships, our health, or anything else that matters to us. Cognitive psychologists have long understood the power of counterfactual thinking. It can serve as a channel of regret, like for Marlon Brando's character in the classic Hollywood film *On the Waterfront*, when he wonders if he might have found greatness in the boxing ring if he hadn't thrown a match that his crooked brother had fixed. Or it can provide a channel of positive reinforcement, assuring us that we made the right choice, such as going on that blind date with someone who ended up becoming your life partner. Recent research by psychology professor Laura Cray of Berkeley and her co-authors argues that counterfactual thinking may even be a key to how people construct a sense of meaning in their lives.

Just as we ask these questions about ourselves, scholars and writers have long speculated on how a whole nation's destiny might have changed if some particular event had or had not happened. Some of the most popular questions hinge on different outcomes to the Second World War. What if Germany had invaded Britain instead of Russia? What if the Japanese hadn't attacked Pearl Harbor? And of direct salience to India, what if the airplane carrying renegade freedom fighter Subhas

Chandra Bose hadn't crashed? Would an Axis victory have hastened or retarded Indian independence?

The uncertainty that all such counterfactuals involve is one big reason why 'serious' historians have tended to avoid them. Interestingly, the one exception is economic history as practised by economists, not historians. Robert Fogel, a Nobel Laureate in Economics and professor at the University of Chicago, wrote a famous study in 1964 in which he analysed the counterfactual of what would have happened to the economy of the US if it hadn't developed a railroad system. The answer, contrary to most people's hunches: not much, because other transportation networks, such as canals and roads, would have expanded instead to fill the gap. Among historians one important exception is the flamboyant and controversial British historian Niall Ferguson, who in 1997 edited a best-selling volume entirely based around counterfactual histories and that, too, written by a collection of eminent historians. As Ferguson rightly argues in his introduction to the volume, all history, except the barest journalistic statement of facts, involves a counterfactual, if only implicitly. Indeed, even a journalistic account of events has to sift the facts and decide which ones are worth presenting and which are trivial: which implicitly involves making a counterfactual judgement on which facts are causally important to the events you're describing and which are incidental and can be safely excluded.

It's often claimed, for example, that British Prime Minister Neville Chamberlain's policy of 'appeasement' towards Adolf Hitler and Nazi Germany was one of the causes of the Second World War. But then this also must mean that if a different policy had been followed, say if Churchill had become prime minister earlier and taken a more aggressive line, the Germans would have seen this as a signal of British strength and would have stepped back from the brink. Under this alternative scenario, war would have been avoided: that's the counterfactual.

Ferguson, never shy of stirring things up, has more recently bluntly argued that the British Empire, especially in its latter, 'benign', phase, was good for its colonies, including India. Among other boons, according to him, the Empire brought free trade, free capital movement, and free movement of people within its orbit, and so helped integrate India more tightly into global commerce and finance. You might even say that the British Empire took the first step in globalizing India, and we're reaping the rewards today. Others, less radical than Ferguson, would point out that, after all, the British brought the English language, law and order, parliamentary democracy, a great railroad system, and gin and beer that are second to none. Prime Minister Manmohan Singh took this more moderate tack in a speech he made at his alma mater Oxford University, while not ignoring the downsides of colonization. And to round out this unlikely trifecta, some Hindu nationalists also argue that British rule was good for India, but for a very different reason. In February 2012, for instance, Mohan Bhagwat, a leader of the Rashtriya Swayamsewak Sangh (RSS), a right-wing Hindu group, argued that India was better off under the British, since post-independence India has seen 'the dominance of rich and powerful people in politics'. Some years ago, a right-wing Hindu ideologue and former Member of Parliament gave one of us a different reason why British rule was better for India's Hindus: 'it got the Muslims off our back', he explained in a moment of candour.

Others, of a more nationalist (or Marxist) bent, say instead, that the British impoverished India and used its wealth and resources to kick-start their Industrial Revolution. Arguing against Ferguson, Nobel Laureate in Economics and fellow Harvard professor Amartya Sen has subtly explored the middle ground, arguing that India *might* have evolved in a different, and possibly better way, if the British hadn't colonized the country. This drew a rejoinder from Ferguson, and a further reply from Sen, all in the pages of the *New Republic* magazine.

So who's right, Sen or Ferguson? Was British rule good for India?

A serious answer to this question has eluded scholars and been mostly a matter of who tells the better story: as it happens, both Sen and Ferguson spin a great yarn. Nor can we observe what would have happened, only what did happen. We don't, alas, have a science fiction time ship we can jump into to explore alternative timelines. Merely looking at the data won't—in fact, *can't*—answer the question. For example, it's commonplace to observe that during the period of British rule, economic growth stagnated, and then took off in the decades following independence. But does this tell us that British rule *caused* India's economic stagnation, and the country would have prospered otherwise? There's no way to tell, unless we come up with a plausible and credible counterfactual history. The trouble is, depending on which one we pick among several plausible-sounding contenders, we get different answers.

For example, if India had slid into civil war, things would probably have turned out much worse than under British rule, and the country might have ended up like present-day Afghanistan. But if a resurgent Mughal (or maybe Maratha?) Empire had revived the country and staged an economic transformation like the Japanese Meiji dynasty, India might be where Japan is today and the world's second richest economy. The debate between Ferguson and Sen hinges, in part, on the plausibility of a 'Meiji India' scenario. Or if the country had managed to keep the British out, but been ruled by a weakened Mughal Empire hemmed in by foreign enclaves and interference, it might have evolved more like China, or maybe Turkey. Or perhaps the country might have been partitioned among the British, French, Portuguese, and Dutch and vanished off the map? We'll never know for sure, but all of us will have our own best guesses on the most likely possibility.

We might never be able to answer the big question of what political configuration might have emerged as an alternative to British rule, but scholarly research can cast light on more specific questions surrounding what British rule in India actually did.

There's certainly suggestive evidence that the British weren't investing as much in India as they were even in their other colonies, nor as much as the parts of India ruled by native princes. Latika Chaudhary, an economics professor at Scripps College in California, has studied the patterns of educational expenditure by the British in India. Her research finds that they spent on average less than one British penny (0.01 Pound

Sterling) per person on education in the regions that they directly controlled. This was half of what the princes spent (about 0.02 Pound). It's also less than the British spent in their other colonies (0.18 Pound). But this by itself isn't conclusive, as it doesn't tell us what the counterfactual scenario would have been under some different system of rule in India.

Lakshmi Iyer, an economics professor at Harvard Business School, has found a clever way to at least get a hint of what the answer might be. She compares the economic performance, post-independence, of those parts of the country which were directly ruled by the British as against those which were ruled by the native princes—the so-called 'princely states'. She shows that the native-ruled regions have done better, on average, than the directly ruled regions. This is because the regions that the British ruled directly even today have a lower level of spending on 'public' goods like schools, hospitals, and roads. Nor are they any better off in terms of investment in agriculture or in productivity growth. Iyer's take is that the British conquered regions with high potential for agricultural cultivation. This makes sense, since rent from land was a big source of revenue for the British in India, as it was for the Mughals before them. This meant that they didn't bother to invest as much in infrastructure and education—what economists call 'physical' and 'human' capital respectively—whereas at least some of the princely states did a good job of investing for the future. The amazing thing is that differences sown a hundred or more years ago are being reaped even today: the regions that were under direct British rule have higher rates of poverty and infant mortality into the present day.

Strikingly, a little more than a century before Iyer's scientific paper, a sharp-eyed observer of colonial India, writing for the *Atlantic*, then as now a leading literary magazine, noted that the princely states of Mysore and Baroda in particular had far better public education than British-ruled India. Jabez T. Sutherland, who seems to be invisible to history except for this prescient essay, writes: 'In these states, particularly Baroda, the people are more free, more prosperous, more contented, and are making more progress, than in any other part of India.' In the years before independence from British rule, Baroda had the good fortune to be ruled by a forward-looking and socially progressive Maharaja named Sayajirao Gaekwad III. During his reign from 1875 to 1939, policies such as compulsory primary education (for girls as well as boys) were put into place. The far-reaching effects of policies such as these are exactly what are picked up by Iyer's research.

Of course, we shouldn't fall into the trap of selection bias ourselves. Mysore, Baroda, and a few other states such as Travancore were exemplary, but there were other princely states that were hardly paragons of good governance. The last Nizam of Hyderabad before the state was absorbed into India possessed a huge fortune in jewels, reportedly making him the richest man in the world, but his personal wealth wasn't necessarily matched by policies that were correspondingly progressive. So it's always tricky to look at one or the other princely state for clues to a general pattern. The point is though, when you crunch the numbers, as Iyer did, the results confirm the intuition that the native-ruled princely states did better, on average, in important ways than the regions the British ruled directly.

Although they're new to history and economics, counterfactual questions have been central to literature and the arts for a long time. Even George Orwell's dystopian masterpiece *Nineteen Eighty-Four* can be read as a counterfactual history of what would have happened if Britain had become a totalitarian state. And science fiction writers love to exploit the possibility of time travel to consider alternate histories. In a classic 'Star Trek' episode, Germany ends up winning the Second World War because an American peace activist who 'should' have been killed in a road accident is miraculously saved by someone from the future. Because of this seemingly minor change in the timeline, America's peace movement manages to delay the US's entry into the Second World War. That gives Germany enough time to complete its heavy water experiments. As an implacable Mr Spock explains the consequences to a horrified Captain Kirk: 'With the A-bomb, and with their V2 rockets to carry them, Germany captured the world.'

If we probe even deeper, thinking counterfactually about history, or our own lives, reinforces a belief in free will. After all, if it had to happen the way it happened, and there was no way it could possibly have happened differently, what's the point of wondering about whether we could have done something else? It would all be karma—or 'causal determinism', in the language of philosophy. If we don't believe in the possibility of a counterfactual, we might as well all be robots, and all of human history would really be the print-out of a sophisticated computer programme set in motion with the 'big bang' that created the universe.

Many important questions, once we unpack them, invoke

a counterfactual. Whether explicitly or not, we're trying to compare the actual world we live in with some alternate world that's different in at least one important detail. The hard part is tracing out the effects of that difference, or our best guess of what might happen. Even if we have a scientific 'model' in our head to guide us, there's always the possibility that random factors—luck—will play a role, and skew our calculations. We can never really *know* for sure what would have happened on the path not taken. The best we can do is speculate, or take an educated guess, on how the journey would have ended up if we'd turned the other way at the fork in the road.

4

Heads or Tails?

I

On February 6, 2004, President of India A.P.J. Abdul Kalam dissolved the Indian Parliament on the advice of Prime Minister Atal Bihari Vajpayee. The economy was booming, the Bharatiya Janata Party (BJP) had fared well in the recent state assembly elections, and the BJP-led National Democratic Alliance (NDA) then in power felt that the momentum was on their side. That might explain why Vajpayee decided to call the elections more than nine months ahead of schedule. Polling took place in four phases between April 20 and May 10. Over 670 million people were eligible to cast a ballot to elect the 543 members of the fourteenth Lok Sabha, the lower house of the Indian Parliament.

Going up against the NDA was the Indian National Congress (INC) party, which had been in the doldrums since losing the 1996 general election. No one gave them much of a chance. Indeed, speaking off the record, several senior Congress leaders told us that they'd more or less resigned themselves to defeat in 2004 as the election campaign unfolded. Early opinion polls augured well for the NDA's chances. On March 27, 2004, an A.C. Neilson poll commissioned by NDTV, a leading cable news channel, and *Indian Express*, a leading daily newspaper, confidently predicted a large majority for the incumbent government. The table below shows how overwhelmingly certain the NDA victory appeared to be.

Table 1

Party/Grouping	NDTV/Indian Express/ A.C. Neilson prediction
NDA	287–307
BJP	190–210
UPA (Congress allies)	143–163
Congress	95–105

Exit polls conducted after the successive rounds of voting see-sawed, but the final exit poll still predicted a majority for the NDA. On the night of May 10, NDA leaders probably went to bed feeling good about their chances. Most people watching the elections whether in India or abroad were convinced too.

When the counting was done, here was the final tally:

Table 2

Party/Grouping	Actual election result
NDA	181
BJP	138
UPA (Congress allies)	216
Congress	145

On May 13, the NDA conceded defeat, and this paved the way for the Congress to form a new government with its own set of allies and take power as the United Progressive Alliance (UPA). This was not only a stunning political reversal, but upended just about everyone's expectations going into the election and through the election process.

The NDA's surprise defeat led to a flurry of Monday morning quarterbacking, with all manner and means of attempts to explain or rationalize the election outcome as well as the wildly inaccurate advance polls. One main storyline emerged, and it's been repeated so many times that it's taken on the aura of gospel truth. According to this received version of things, it's the poor and marginalized voters, both the rural and the urban poor, who punished the NDA for its triumphalist 'India Shining' election campaign. The alliance's appeal to India's recent economic and other successes on the world stage, so the narrative runs, backfired with those who felt they'd been left out of the India growth miracle. They showed up in droves to vote the government out of office, and that's the story.

It wasn't just the usual suspects such as left-wing commentators—who would have welcomed the fact that the BJP's pro-market policies were the reason for their defeat—that bought into this interpretation. Even the BJP's senior leaders admitted that 'India Shining' had backfired and they'd failed to communicate their message about India's economic progress to the voters, and that five years was too short a time span to achieve equitable economic development.

As compelling as this narrative is, there's one main problem with it: it happens to be wrong. Take a look at this Table:

Table 3

Grouping	Popular vote (change)	Seats (change)	Seat/Popular vote ratio
NDA	33.3% (-3.76%)	181 (-89)	5.4
UPA (Congress allies)	35.4% (+7.1%)	216 (+83)	6.1

What emerges paints a very different picture from Tables 1 and 2. There was a difference between the two major groupings in the share of popular vote of just fractionally more than 2 per cent. While it's true that that there was a 'swing' (polling jargon for the change from last time) in favour of the Congress and its allies and against the NDA, that still adds up to a tiny difference in the national popular vote. Here's the crux: in a 'first past the post' system, it's not the popular vote share, but the seats you win that count. Look at the last column of Table 3. The Congress and its allies got a little more than six seats for every percentage of popular vote they earned; the NDA got less than five and a half seats. That's the story. The 2 per cent difference in popular vote, magnified by the Congress and its allies getting more bang for the buck in converting votes into seats, won the day.

Here's another way of looking at it. The bottom line is that the NDA and the UPA each got about a third of the votes cast, with the remaining third going to the many small regional parties (plus the left parties) which weren't allied to either large bloc. Put that way, it hardly looks like a stunning defeat. Rather, there was a small swing away from the NDA, and, unfortunately for them, it cost them big time. In fact, they could still have won, if not for the fact that a crucial ally, the Dravida Munnetra Kazagham (DMK), a regional party from Tamil Nadu, switched allegiances at the last minute. Their 16 seats made all the difference in the end. With the DMK, the NDA would have come back to power, albeit with a slim majority; without them, they were doomed. So that explains why the NDA lost. Yet the conventional story is so gripping and feeds our desire to have a convincing explanation for the BJP's defeat when the truth is it might just have been bad luck.

Yogendra Yadav is a political scientist and expert pollster at the Centre for the Study of Developing Societies (CSDS) in Delhi and knows the perils and pitfalls of polls better than most. CSDS runs polls for the *Indian Express*, a leading daily, and CNN-IBN, a leading cable news channel. Yadav's polls are probably the best in the business. As it happens, he didn't poll during the 2004 general election and was one of the few pollsters that year not to get egg on his face.

Yadav believes polls in India have improved in the last 20 years—in quantity, if not in quality. Unlike his polls, which are based on a sound statistical methodology that's available for scrutiny by scholars or the public, most polls in the Indian media don't reveal their methodology. Especially problematic, in Yadav's view, is that they don't make public the demographic characteristics of the people they polled, nor for that matter is there any assurance that the sample was anywhere close to random. Further, they don't explain the mapping they used from vote share to projected seats won. That doesn't stop anyone, of course, from splashing them across newspapers or TV screens.

Folks who study polls, like Yadav, identify three major reasons why they can go wrong. The first reason is what statisticians call 'sampling error'. To be accurate, a poll should sample randomly from the pool of voters, the aim being to get a representative slice of the electorate. But pollsters aren't always able to get truly random samples and this can skew the results. Here's a simple example. Suppose a naïve pollster wanders into a constituency and asks the first person they meet to round up 10 of their buddies because they want to ask them how they just voted. If unbeknownst to the pollster, this stranger happens to be an organizer for one of the parties and they get ten party workers in for the pollster to talk to, it's not hard to guess the huge bias the sampling error would cause.

It's possible to minimize though not eliminate this source of error by picking a truly random sample such as going through voter lists. This is in fact what the CSDS pollsters try to do, but even then there's no guarantee that your sample would be truly representative. The danger, not just in India, but in most places, is that samples will over-represent well to do or better connected people and under-represent the poor and the marginalized. For example, a middle class housewife might be at home and available to be polled but an agricultural labourer might be in the fields all day and miss out on being polled. This kind of problem is especially acute for non-random samples, like with exit polls where the pollster is talking to folks leaving the polling station. The selection of people who have the time and leisure to stick around and talk to the pollster compared to those who head directly back home or to work isn't likely to be representative, much less random.

There's widespread agreement that sampling error was one of the main reasons why the polls wrongly called the 2004 elections for the NDA. As Yadav explains, urban middle class voters were heavily oversampled in 2004 compared to the rural poor. They were simply easier for the city slicker pollsters to get hold of. The problem this caused is pretty obvious to anyone who realizes that the BJP's core support comes from the urban middle class, whereas the Congress draws its greatest strength from the poor, especially the rural poor, and minorities. So this sampling bias showed the BJP getting more support than they were actually getting. If the pollsters had spoken to a truly representative group of people, they would have figured out that the BJP's support wasn't as high as their non-random sample of voters surveyed seemed to suggest. In that sense, Yadav believes the 2004 election was a 'special' case in that the sampling bias was so severe.

The second source of error is called 'response bias'. In simple terms people might not be truthful when they speak to pollsters. Take Uttar Pradesh, India's most populous state and, if it were a country, the world's fourth largest democracy. Politics and identity have long been intertwined in this large, poor state in the heartland of north India. Many voters in UP tend to pick the party they support along the lines of their own caste or ethnic identities. So for example, the Bahujan Samaj Party (BSP) champions the Dalits (lower-caste Hindus formerly known as 'untouchables') and draws its greatest support from this community. But the BSP also gets some support from upper caste voters. Suppose a pollster spoke to one of them, but they were embarrassed to admit that they voted for a 'low-caste party', and so lied to the pollster. There's response bias for you.

The third source of error is one spotted in the context of the 2004 election, which is translating popular vote shares into seats actually won. In a proportional representation system like in many European countries, parties are allotted seats directly in proportion to the share of the votes they receive, with parliamentarians being selected from a pre-determined party list. But, in a British or Westminster-style system with single-winner constituencies, in which the winner needs only a plurality, not a majority, of the vote, there's isn't an automatic or mechanical relationship between votes and seats—exactly as we saw with the 2004 results. This system is used in Britain and most Commonwealth countries, including India, as well as for elections to the US Congress. The system is often called 'first past the post' in the British context or 'winner takes all' in the American context.

In two party systems like in the US, this is less of a problem because the vote share is usually a good predictor of the number of seats either major party is going to win: if you win a bigger share of the votes, chances are you'll win the seat. But in India, which often has three or four parties as viable contenders in any given constituency, extrapolating from state-wide or national vote shares to the number of seats any party might win is very treacherous. A party which has a lot of support, but which is thinly spread across constituencies, will do badly, vote for vote, compared to a party whose support is heavily concentrated. This is exactly what throws off poll predictions in complex and 'multi-cornered' elections as frequently happen in UP.

In Yadav's exacting professional judgement—don't forget that he's a scholar as well as a pollster—his own polls, widely acknowledged to be the best, aren't yet good enough. What is the reason for this? It's because we don't know whether the errors cancel each other out or instead 'add up' to give us a really bad prediction, and what would explain this. Whether it was the television pundits in the US confidently predicting that Al Gore had won the 2000 Presidential election to all the pollsters who'd called the NDA's victory in 2004, polls are usually wrong as many times as they're right.

The bottom line is that polls are most accurate when there's a wide margin separating the different political parties. When races are tight, and especially when there are many parties in the running, they're much less accurate. In other words, polls are least reliable when they'd be most useful.

But don't take our word on it. Even Yogendra Yadav admits that polls often fail to predict election results accurately. If polls are misleading, should we look instead to the judgement of experts?

II

Sure, India could be a dangerous place for women. Whether it's domestic violence, neglect of the girl child, sex-selective abortion, or the continuing prevalence of dowry, all of which are widely reported almost every day, life in India does seem tough for its women. But is it worse than in other countries we suspect might also be dangerous for women? Can you quantify such things?

In June 2011, newspapers carried the headline that India is, in fact, the 'fourth most dangerous' country in the world for women. It was just ahead of Somalia. Afghanistan was the worst, followed by the Democratic Republic of Congo and Pakistan. What was this conclusion based on? Was it an analysis of the relevant statistics that were compiled into an index? No. It was based on a survey of 213 experts conducted by TrustLaw, a service providing information on women's rights that's run by the Thomson Reuters Foundation. The experts spanned the spectrum from academics, aid professionals, journalists, policymakers, and development specialists. They were asked for their opinion on what they thought the most dangerous places in the world were, with a series of separate follow-up questions on dimensions of women's safety such as health, access to economic resources, cultural or religious discrimination, sexual violence, and the risk of being subjected to human trafficking.

The final number was arrived at by adding together and weighing the responses of all of these experts. So, would it be correct to say that a survey found India to be the fourth most dangerous place in the world for women? No. A more accurate, though less spicy, way of putting it would be that among a survey of experts, India showed up in fourth place when these experts' opinions on how dangerous different countries are for women were added together. It doesn't necessarily mean that, in any statistically meaningful sense, India (or any other country) is actually fourth (or first, or tenth) most dangerous. A survey like this is only as valuable as the level of faith you put in experts and the methodology of adding opinions together into one composite number.

Psychological research tells us that human beings instinctively dislike uncertainty. We want definite answers to questions that are intrinsically difficult to tackle. We like easily digestible and understandable information, such as lists of the 'Top 10': whether it's billionaires or most dangerous countries. Information that helps us understand and analyse our difficult world is particularly sought after, especially if it's cloaked in the garb of expert truth. If you've watched toothpaste ads, you'll recall seeing the virtues of this or the other toothpaste brand being extolled by a serious-looking 'expert' (usually an actor, the fine print tells you) clad in a white lab coat. And don't forget the talking heads on TV, who are almost always well groomed and snazzily dressed, as if that had anything to do with the quality of their information or insight.

And if understanding the present weren't hard enough, we also want to know what's going to happen in the future, whether it's the outcome of an election, the performance of the stock market, or our own personal futures. Often, the real test of expertise is a prediction about the future. Any reasonably intelligent person should be able to look backward and form a judgement, but it's left up to the 'real' experts to be able to look forward into the future and make predictions about it, aspiring to an omniscience once reserved for the gods.

From astrology to tarot, human history is littered with our attempts at better predicting the future. More recently, these include more scientific (or at least apparently so) methods like polls and expert predictions. But as our look back at the 2004 Indian election just showed us, pundits and pollsters often get it badly wrong.

Philip Tetlock, a psychology professor at the University of Pennsylvania, is most famous for a 20-year study in which he tracked the predictions of hundreds of experts in many different fields spanning the range from business to international relations and then compared the actual outcomes to the predictions. He published his results in a landmark 2005 book called *Expert Political Judgement: How Good Is It? How Can We Know?* It was a year too late to help the pundits and prognosticators who had been so badly off in predicting the 2004 Indian election. In the study, he found that the predictions of experts were no more accurate than if you'd just tossed a coin instead. In fact, sometimes tossing a coin would give you a better prediction than listening to an expert. As Tetlock colourfully puts it, even a monkey throwing darts at a dartboard would do better than most experts. You could probably do even better than the monkey, but that would be just by mechanically extrapolating a trend from today into the future. (The simplest form of extrapolation is what's known in mathematics as 'linear extrapolation'. Basically, if you have two points, you put a straight line through those points and make a prediction assuming that the next data point will also lie along that same straight line.)

There are innumerable examples of what Tetlock has in mind. Here's one from March 2012. A much publicized paper by economics professor Dan Johnson of Colorado College and Ayfer Ali created a complicated statistical model with many variables to predict how countries would do in the medal tally of the winter and summer Olympic Games. They have a very large data set spanning games from 1952 to the present. The authors find some interesting correlations between variables, such as the intuitive ideas that rich countries win more medals than poor countries and that countries with snowy winters do better in the winter games. Where they falter is when they claim that their statistical model can provide 'surprisingly accurate predictions' of medal tallies in future games. But as Roger Pielke Jr, a professor of environmental studies at the University of Colorado, Boulder, showed, the interesting correlations that Johnson and Ali found didn't translate into good predictive power. In line with Tetlock's research, Pielke showed that the naïve assumption that a country would win as many medals next time as last time performs better than the complicated statistical model.

The news doesn't get any better. If statistical models perform poorly at making predictions, experts do even worse. Tetlock identifies two main types of experts, depending on their personalities, the first being 'hedgehogs', single-minded devotees to a particular big concept or idea, which they stick to through thick or thin. While performing worst of all, they also tend to be the experts with the highest media profile, whether it's conventional media such as newspapers and TV or social media such as Twitter and the blogosphere. Such people exude confidence, don't mince words, and boldly tell you what's going to happen. More often than not, they're wrong. The second type of expert, who does a little better than tossing a coin and that, too, way better than the hedgehogs, are what Tetlock calls the 'foxes'. Foxes are pragmatic and not ideological. They're willing to change their minds, or even discard a cherished theory, if the facts point in a different direction. Foxes are circumspect, cautious, and will make predictions only grudgingly, knowing well that the chances are high that they might be wrong. Not surprisingly these are the folks you don't see as the talking heads on TV. The wisdom of a fox doesn't translate into a good sound bite or a 140-character tweet like the certainty of a hedgehog does.

Despite Tetlock's well-publicized and much discussed research, which has been popularized and extended in Dan Gardner's book, *Future Babble*, surveys based on expert opinions of dubious value, to say nothing of ubiquitous expert commentary, are still trotted out and garner much media attention. A fiercely competitive media environment, as in India or the US, which places a heavy premium on sounding and looking confident while pontificating, accentuates this tilt towards hedgehogs. In the battle for public attention, the bold, if reckless, predictions of a confident hedgehog are an easier sell than the thoughtful fox who tells you that they don't really know what's going to happen. If the predictions match the ideological persuasion of the TV host or the intended audience, so much the better. Yogendra Yadav, the polling guru, believes this is one reason why the quality of political punditry in India hasn't improved although the quantity has exploded.

The advent of social media in India, especially Twitter, Facebook and blogs, has definitely democratized the channels of communication between those who want to get their views out and those who're looking to be informed and engage in a dialogue. In the old media, an expert commentator will usually have the right institutional connection, the right family background, or be well-networked—often all three.

In the social media, anyone with a computer and an internet connection can proclaim themselves an expert. Ironically, the welter of so many new voices competing for attention has, if anything, increased the premium on being a hedgehog and made the foxes even more invisible than before. If you have to be strong, decisive, and articulate in a two-minute sound bite on television, it's exponentially more important when you have to get your point across in 140 characters. The medium isn't given to nuances. At least in India, if you'd like to have your voice heard on Twitter, turning into a hedgehog is your best bet.

III

If polls are so unreliable, why do we rely on them so much? And when an election outcome turns out differently than we expected, or even if it confirms our expectations, why are we so eager to provide a neat theory which explains what happened? You would think that after so many faulty predictions, the experts would realize the jig is up and take down their shingle, or they'd be fired by the news organizations.

A superficial answer is that since there's a demand for prediction, even ones that turn out to be wrong, there's going to be a supply. Economics doesn't get more basic than demand and supply. But that begs the deeper questions: why is prediction so tough and why are we so often mistaken? Leaving aside the errors of experts and pundits, even the most scientific of statistical predictions—like opinion polls—are wrong at least as often as they are right. Even the best predictive model, in the end, doesn't do much better than tossing a coin. So why do we keep at it?

To borrow the title of the best-selling book by Nassim Taleb, we're 'fooled by randomness'. He argues compellingly that the world around us is in many ways unknowable. At a deep level, modern quantum mechanics tells us the same thing. According to the 'Heisenberg uncertainty principle', we can't simultaneously observe the position and the trajectory of a subatomic (quantum) particle. By fixing one of them, we disturb the other. In other words, observation is intimately intertwined with our objective reality, which at the most fundamental subatomic level is impossible to pin down with any certainty. What's true for subatomic particles is also true in the world that affects us directly as humans. In tennis, the fate of a match could be decided by whether a tennis ball topples forward or drops back when it hits the top of the net. That might make the difference between becoming a champion and winding up a runner-up. Yet, as Taleb argues, humans can't accept that reality is chaotic, and are always looking, at least subconsciously, for ways to rationalize and explain it—such as the sports cliché that 'champions make their own luck'.

Expert predictions and, in the case of elections, polls, are two ways to do that. More fundamentally, Taleb suggests, we're wrongly attributing a cause-and-effect chain of circumstances to events when, in fact, so much of what happens is fundamentally random and impossible to neatly parcel into cause and effect. We see something random, and then we come up with an explanation that's little more than a rationalization after the fact. In a bigger sense, we love to see patterns, and infer mechanisms that lie behind them, when we often ought to be seeing chaos, complexity, and randomness. Our ancestors in all cultures looked up at the night sky, but rather than seeing a chaotic bunch of dots, they saw the shapes that became the signs of the zodiac.

A trader by profession, Taleb's most persuasive examples come from financial markets. The failure of most economists and financial experts to predict the global financial crisis that started in 2007 is the most obvious recent case in point. Yet, the story of the 2004 election we've looked at fits perfectly. As we saw, the received wisdom tells us that it was a vote against the NDA's economic policies. Yet another standard tack is that it represents an 'anti-incumbency' vote. A third theory might be that it was a vote in favour of the Congress' policy platform geared toward the 'aam aadmi' (common man). Yet none of these stories really stand up to scrutiny: they're all interesting ideas, but you couldn't prove or disprove any or all of them based on the election results. And a theory that can't be either proved or disproved isn't really a theory, it's more like religion.

Let's take another look at Table 4.

Table 4

Grouping	Popular vote (change)	Seats (change)	Seat/Popular vote ratio
NDA	33.3% (–3.76%)	181 (–89)	5.4
UPA (Congress allies)	35.4% (+7.1%)	216 (+83)	6.1

The NDA's defeat all boiled down to a 2 per cent difference in the vote share compared to the Congress and its allies. That's less than the margin of error of any poll. In other words, it's so small a gap that it's just as easily explained as purely the result of random factors as it is by any of these sophisticated cause-and-effect theories. It was decided by a coin toss. All of these theories that claim vindication based on their reading of the 2004 elections are like a row of grand mansions built on quicksand.

There's a principle in logic called 'Occam's razor'. It says: When trying to explain something, use the most parsimonious explanation you can think of. Prefer the simple to the complicated. Be economical. If we were applying that logic to the 2004 election, and we had the humility of a fox rather than the preconceptions of a hedgehog, we'd say that, based on the data, the election outcome was the result of unforeseeable random factors. It's as if someone had tossed a coin, 'heads' the NDA wins, 'tails' Congress wins. The coin came up tails. End of story. There's no big 'lesson' to take to the bank, write into the history books, or build theories about.

You might have hoped that we'd have learned something since then. We haven't. The big regional election in 2012 was the assembly election in Uttar Pradesh in the month of March. The issue here wasn't so much the polls, which all agreed that the Bahujan Samaj Party (BSP) would go down to defeat at the hands of the Samajwadi Party (SP). What took everyone by surprise was the magnitude of the BSP's defeat and the SP's victory. Predictably, in the immediate aftermath of the election, newspaper op-eds, TV talk shows and social media such as

Twitter were full of analysis on why the BSP had lost. Noted commentators weighed in with the confidence of hedgehogs. There were three main theories put forward.

The first was that it was a vote for development and against UP's traditional identity politics. Supporters of this theory pointed to the pro-development bits of the SP's platform and the claim that voters were reacting in disgust at the alleged corruption of the BSP government, especially of Chief Minister Mayawati.

The second main explanation was the opposite. It was the triumph of old-fashioned identity politics and a failure to move toward the development-oriented politics of Bihar or Gujarat. Supporters of this theory pointed to the fact that the SP and the BSP were relying on the support of their traditional vote banks and there was nothing really development-oriented about the SP's platform.

The third school of thought dusted off the old chestnut that it was an anti-incumbency bias. In 2007, the BSP had ousted the SP, so the 2012 election was just the pendulum swinging back the other way.

These theories all sound good. (In the interests of full disclosure we should tell you that Rupa devoted her weekly column in the *Wall Street Journal India* to an explanation of the UP election result based on the second theory. Well-known commentators in the *Indian Express* and the *Economic Times* went for the first theory. A well-known commentator in the *Wall Street Journal* opted for a combination of the second and third.) Which one is right? Take a look at Table 5.

Table 5

Party	Popular vote (%)	Seats (out of 403)	Seat share (%)	Seat/Popular vote ratio
SP	29.3	226	56	7.7
BSP	25.9	80	19.8	3.1
BJP	15	47	11.7	3.1
INC	11.7	28	6.9	2.4
RLD	2.3	9	2.2	3.9

Despite all of the hype about the BSP's collapse and the SP's triumphant resurgence, the difference in popular vote was a measly 3.4 per cent. What really crucified the BSP was the magnifying effect of the SP's popular vote into seats. Look at the last column. For every 1 per cent of the vote the BSP got, it won a little more than three seats. The BJP, Congress and Rashtriya Lok Dal (RLD, another small party) were in the same ball park. But the SP got a whopping eight seats for every 1 per cent of popular vote. It was sweet revenge, because in 2007 the oddities of the vote to seat translation gave the BSP an overwhelming victory with again a small difference in popular vote.

Even more than the 2004 general election, the 2012 UP election is a story of a slender victory margin greatly magnified by a Westminster-style voting system. We do need to be a little cautious. A three per cent or four per cent difference in vote shares, as between the SP and the BSP, isn't trivially small in a parliamentary democracy. While that difference may be too large to be totally random, and might, in jargon, be 'statistically significant', it's way too small a difference on which to build a grand theory about epochal change in UP politics. Truth be told, it can just as easily and more parsimoniously be attributed to a combination of randomness and a small percentage of voters ditching the BSP in favour of the SP for one reason or another. As we see it, you might just as well explain it by saying that the political gods tossed a coin and it came up in favour of the SP, rather than sign on to any of these fancy cause-and-effect theories. The theories are little more than a Rorschach ink blot test that tells us more about the political pundits than they do about what they're claiming to analyse. But that never stopped anyone.

While Yogendra Yadav wouldn't go quite as far as we did with this claim, he did concede that it's impossible to confirm or disprove any of these theories on the basis of the actual election results or any of the polls. You can never know, after all, exactly why someone voted the way they did. In his words, the analyst has to take a 'causal leap' in moving from the facts of the election result to an interpretation of why it happened. But Yadav is a rare fox in a forest of hedgehogs.

As India begins to gear up for the next general election as we write this in late 2012, watch out for all those gathering hedgehogs and proliferating opinion polls, and do keep that dart-throwing monkey in the back of your mind.

IV

In 1965, a boy met a girl at a Greek restaurant in Cambridge, England. It was the sort of place popular with students that serves tasty food at reasonable prices, especially with international students, living in an era before chicken tikka masala became the national dish and English cuisine was impossibly bland. Like Romeo and Juliet, it was love at first sight. The young couple went steady and finally married in 1968. After that they moved in with the boy's mother.

In and of itself, there's nothing unusual about a story like this. It happens all the time. What makes it different is that this young couple came from such different backgrounds. The boy was as blue-blooded as they come, from a privileged Indian family. The girl came from a very modest background, from a small town in Italy. He was in Cambridge attending the university, where members of his family had studied for several generations. She was in Cambridge not at the fabled university but taking English language classes at a private college. He came from a political family, whereas her father was a humble stone mason.

That they met when and where they did was a matter of pure chance. If they'd come to Cambridge even a few years apart they probably would never have met. If either one of them didn't fancy Greek food, or hadn't gone out that evening, they might never have met. But through a twist of fate they did, in fact, meet and the rest, as they say, is history.

If you know recent Indian history, by now you've probably guessed that he was Rajiv Gandhi and she was Antonia Maino, whom you probably know better as Sonia Gandhi.

Look at the series of random and unpredictable occurrences that it took even after they met and married to bring Sonia Gandhi to 10 Janpath, her official residence in Delhi as the head of the governing Indian National Congress party and by any account one of the most powerful women in the world. For one thing, Rajiv was never destined for politics. He was a commercial airline pilot and didn't have political aspirations. His younger brother, Sanjay, his mother Indira Gandhi's favourite, was being groomed to succeed her. His untimely death at the age of 33 when the plane he was piloting came down in flames near Safdarjung airport in Delhi on June 23, 1980 changed everything. The reluctant Rajiv was drafted into politics. Even then he was a reticent and unwilling politician. History took another unexpected turn when Indira Gandhi was assassinated by her Sikh bodyguards on October 31, 1984, in revenge for her government's putdown of the Sikh insurgency in Punjab. That led Rajiv into the prime minister's chair. Through the vicissitudes of his political career, Sonia remained entirely in the background. Even after Rajiv Gandhi's assassination on May 21, 1991, she declined to jump into the fray and stayed out of politics for the next decade and a half. It wasn't until the Congress's unexpected victory that we've talked about, in 2004, that she stepped into public life as the head of the UPA.

But even this wasn't a pre-ordained conclusion. As observed by writer and historian Patrick French in his 2011 book, *India: An Intimate Biography of 1.2 Billion People*, it took another series of unexpected deaths of senior Congress leaders for Sonia to ascend to the party's top job. As French writes:

> *Then, in an extraordinary series of coincidences, the internal opposition [to Sonia] within the Congress party disappeared. In June 2000, Rajesh Pilot died when his*

> *car collided with a Rajasthan State Road Transport bus; in October 2000, Sitaram Kesri passed away following a heart attack; in January 2001, the 62-year-old Jitendra Prasada suffered a sudden and fatal brain haemorrhage; in September 2001, Madhavrao Scindia was flying to Kanpur in an industrialist's Cessna C-90 for a state election rally when the plane abruptly fell out of the sky. After this, dissent stopped: the challengers were gone.*

To put it in somewhat grisly terms, Sonia's journey from a shy Italian housewife to the most powerful person in India took two assassinations and five unexpected deaths after her chance meeting with her future husband. While it's impossible to calculate, the odds would be so stacked against such a possibility as to be almost zero.

We're so used to life unfolding in a predictable way through a series of linked cause-and-effect relationships that we're apt to forget the overwhelming role of random chance in our lives. The story of Sonia Gandhi is just one of the most remarkable reminders of this fact. But if you think about it, it's not hard to see how random events—by which we mean events and circumstances entirely beyond our control—so powerfully affect our lives. This is a point that's been vividly brought out in Malcolm Gladwell's best-selling book, *Outliers*. Often the biggest of these are the place and time where you were born, something over which you have absolutely no control. The life prospects of someone born in a rich country of the West are many times greater than someone born in a poor country like India, except for the tiny fraction of the rich elite. And a person who enters the job market during an economic boom has much greater earning and career prospects than another person who enters the job market in a recession.

When and where you were born are, of course, the big ones, but any number of random occurrences could have a huge impact on your life. Consider the plight of refugee claimants in a country such as Canada, which is known for being compassionate toward refugees. Even then, claimants have to wait for years for their cases to be decided. You'd think that when a case comes up for review, it would be decided purely on its merits: that someone deserving of refugee status would be granted it, whereas a frivolous applicant or would-be economic migrant would be denied. Think again.

A March 2012 study by Sean Rehaag, a law professor at Osgoode Hall in Toronto, pored over more than 23,000 applications for a judicial review of refugee claims that were filed before the Canadian Federal Courts between 2005 and 2010. Cases get to the Federal Court when an initial claim by a refugee has been turned down by the government board which administers them. A review by a Federal judge is often a refugee's last shot at remaining in Canada and not being deported to their home country. And that could be a very grim fate, if your home country lies in a war zone or you've fled persecution, pestilence, or famine. Rehaag's study revealed that, on average, Federal judges grant a leave to remain in Canada only about 14.4 per cent of the time. What's shocking is the huge variation in the propensity of particular judges to grant leave. They vary from a tiny 1.36 per cent to an enormous 78 per cent with the whole range in between. Another way of looking at it is that on the toss of a coin a refugee claimant whose case came up before the most lenient judge would be 57.33 times more likely to be allowed to stay than another refugee who came up before the stingiest judge. If you're a refugee in Canada, this is depressing news. It means that Tetlock's proverbial monkey with the dart is deciding your fate.

Economists who study labour markets have tried for a long time to parse the role of luck in people's career prospects. And philosophers think about this too. If a billionaire's fortune was entirely the result of pure luck rather than their skill or ability, society would take a different view on whether it was desirable or wise to tax it away. Most people except for diehard left-wingers would agree that someone should keep the money they've earned through the sweat of their brow, but all except the extreme libertarians would say that it's legitimate to tax windfall gains that are the result of pure chance—say through winning a lottery or inheritance. Intuitively, as human beings, we're more apt to think that someone deserves something when they get it through their own effort and ability rather than having it handed to them on a silver platter with watercress round it.

Certainly, many people seem to believe that luck has played a big role in their careers. While definitely not scientific (we haven't forgotten that we told you what we think about surveys), it's at least suggestive that in a survey of 7,000 members of the professional social network LinkedIn, a staggering 84 per cent agreed that luck factors in to how well they do at work. In an Indian counterpart, of 500 or more business professionals surveyed on LinkedIn, 79 per cent thought that luck was important in their careers. Again, we should note that 500 isn't large enough to make a statistically valid claim about what all Indian professionals might think. Plus, there's the issue of selection, since by definition people who don't use LinkedIn couldn't express their opinion, or perhaps those who felt more passionately were more likely to respond. But there's one major difference between a survey like this and a survey of experts. This survey doesn't purport to find that luck is actually important, just people's subjective assessments of the importance of luck. That's a much more modest claim than saying, for example, that any particular country is the most dangerous place for one or the other group.

The trouble is this: in the context of labour markets, it's very hard to separate out the effect of luck as compared to innate ability. Worldwide, the biggest factor that determines your career prospects and lifetime earnings is the quality of your education. A Harvard graduate, on average, will do better than a graduate of a state university, and, in India, an Indian Institutes of Technology (IIT) or Indian Institutes of Management (IIM) graduate will do better than a graduate from a generic engineering or business school. But getting into a top school is a function both of ability and luck. So it's hard to know for any given person what was more important.

Likewise, in sports, success is a function of some combination of skill and luck, which is difficult to disentangle. Winning a major tennis championship, for example, obviously requires great skill, but also a few lucky breaks, such as a net court going in your favour during a crucial game. In sports, though, it's sometimes possible to get at the effect of pure luck and trace its effects through a sportsman's career. In many sports, playing at home confers an advantage over playing away. This 'home field' advantage has many sources, and is universally acknowledged by sportsmen and by sports fans. It can be as simple as the testosterone spike you get from having the home fans cheer you on to something as subtle as a more intimate knowledge of home playing conditions than your visiting opponents would have.

In some team sports, the home field advantage might be purely the psychological boost of being at home. For example, at least in theory, an ice hockey rink should be identical whether it's in Ottawa, Canada, or in Los Angeles, California, since it's maintained in a controlled environment and the speed of the puck on the ice is regulated. But sports played outdoors, in which atmospheric conditions and the responsiveness of the playing surface are important, confer a more specific and not purely psychological home field advantage. This is true whether it's soccer, baseball, tennis, or golf. But it's especially true in India's favourite sport, cricket. Unlike in baseball, where the pitcher tosses the ball directly at the batter without it hitting the ground (in cricket parlance, a 'full toss', which is rare), the cricket bowling action requires the bowler to run forward and then bounce the ball off the playing surface, known as the pitch. The condition of the pitch is best attuned to a particular style of bowling, and humidity in the atmosphere affects how much the ball bounces off the pitch and swings in the air. Plus, temperature and humidity affect the condition both of the pitch and the outfield. Most cricket aficionados would agree that this confers a huge home field advantage.

So where does luck come in? For a cricketer playing at the highest level, which is international test cricket played between national sides, the one thing he can't control is where he makes his debut. The schedule of test matches among the playing nations is fixed months and years in advance. So when a new player makes his debut on the world stage, it'll be purely luck of the draw whether he debuts at home or abroad. It's common sense to believe that this would affect his performance in the debut series. But could where you debut have a long-lasting impact on your performance as an international test cricketer? If so, something totally random at the start of your career could affect you until the very end.

Shekhar Aiyar and Rodney Ramcharan, economists at the International Monetary Fund in Washington, DC, wanted to investigate this possibility systematically. In a study released in March 2011, they constructed data on all test cricketers who debuted between 1950 and 1985 to find out if where they debuted did, in fact, have a long lasting impact. Not surprisingly, they found that in the debut series itself, there was a huge effect. Batsmen on average had a 33 per cent higher batting average and bowlers about an 18 per cent lower bowling average. To put that in perspective, that's the difference between a superstar and a middling player. What's more surprising is that Aiyar and Ramcharan found a persistent impact on where you debuted over the entire career of a test cricketer, although as you'd expect, the effect was attenuated over time. Still the effect isn't small: a 10 per cent higher debut score translated into a 5 per cent better overall career productivity.

What accounts for these long-lasting impacts of where you

debuted? There are two main possibilities. The first is that debuting under favourable conditions at home could help a player hone his skills and these could remain important over his whole career. For example, batsmen debuting at home could develop better technique and confidence because they're less likely to be bowled out on their familiar home surface. The second main possibility is that selectors—those who pick the test teams—might unfairly penalize players who debuted abroad and scored poorly compared to those who debuted at home. The bottom line is that both of these things are probably happening and together help explain why debuting at home is so important.

Examples abound of cricketers who debuted at home and went on to spectacular test careers. Among batsmen, Aiyar suggests, think of Mohammad Azharuddin; as for bowlers, look at B.S. Chandrashekhar. It's harder to think of promising cricketers who debuted abroad and didn't live up to their potential. But there's an obvious reason for that. As Shekhar Aiyar explains to us, many promising players debuting abroad got dropped from the national side and so never had the opportunity to become household names, unlike the luckier players who debuted at home: that's why it's tough to name them.

It's a sobering thought. For every one person who got lucky and made it big, there are thousands of others who didn't quite make the cut through no fault of their own. Then there's the spectacular randomness of being at the right place at the right time, like at a particular Greek restaurant in Cambridge, England on a particular day in 1965. All of that randomness at the level of us individuals doesn't add up nicely into a smooth and predictable world. Even elections in which hundreds of millions of people vote, basically wind up being determined by a coin toss. The human condition is irreducibly random. Just ask Atal Bihari Vajpayee.

5

Mythical or Modern?

I

Even fans of Steven Spielberg's *Indiana Jones* movie franchise will candidly admit that the second instalment, *Indiana Jones and the Temple of Doom*, from 1984, represents a low point in the saga. The film's depiction of a bloodthirsty cult devoted to the Hindu goddess Kali was seen as so offensive that the Indian government didn't allow Spielberg to film in India, so they shot the movie in Sri Lanka instead. It may not have gone down well in the movie, but the fascination of ancient temples and the huge riches they might contain is an old one.

Indy usually finds the treasure with the help of his trusty whip, and an attractive blonde by his side, but in the summer of 2011, in the city of Thiruvananthapuram in the state of Kerala, the weapon of choice was a court order and the protagonist an ageing lawyer. In 2007, the lawyer, T.P. Sundararajan, filed a case in court against the administrators of the Sri Padmanabhaswamy temple in Thiruvananthapuram claiming that it was being mismanaged by the private trust that ran it. The trust was headed by Marthanda Varma, the head of the Travancore royal family whose ancestors had built the temple and run it for centuries.

After a lengthy legal battle, searchers sent by the court went to inspect the secret vaults hidden behind the temple's sanctum sanctorum. On June 30, 2011, they opened the first of the vaults ('A') and discovered an enormous treasure trove of gold, jewels, and ornaments made of pure gold and encrusted with jewels. No one knows exactly how much it's worth but estimates put it at a staggering $22 billion. The searchers couldn't open the second vault ('B'), which was jammed shut, and a further court order has prevented it from being opened so far. At the time we write this, in 2012, an inventory of the riches inside vault 'A' had just begun and vault 'B' remained sealed. Some people speculate it contains even vaster riches but Marthanda Varma has denied this and no one really knows.

The value of the treasure at Sri Padmanabhaswamy temple was larger than anyone could have possibly imagined. To put things in perspective, the GDP of the state of Kerala was about $6 billion in 2011. In other words, the contents of just one of the vaults in the temple is worth more than three and a half times what the entire state of Kerala produces in a year! Or think about it this way. If Marthanda Varma owned the contents of vault 'A', he'd be slightly richer than the hedge fund manager George Soros and the steel tycoon Lakshmi Mittal, and just slightly below the industrialist Mukesh Ambani, according to the 2012 Forbes 400 list of the world's richest people.

The relationship between gold and jewels on the one hand and Hindu temples on the other is an ancient one. The great temples, especially in south India which remained relatively immune from Islamic invaders who swept into north India, remain to this day repositories of great wealth. All of the great temples in medieval south India, many of which remain in active worship, had royal patrons who erected and supported them. On festive occasions or after a major military victory, royal patrons bestowed riches in the form of gold, jewels, or icons (sometimes made of gold and encrusted with jewels) on 'their' temple. Regular devotees, too, would give gifts to the temple as a sign of their devotion: what goes for Maharajas goes for normal people too. Traditionally, in the days before banks and the stock market, families saved their wealth in the form of gold and jewellery, which were also used as a form of ritual offering to temples. That tradition continues to this day.

Dhanteras is the first day of the Hindu festival of Diwali. It's a day on which Lakshmi, the Hindu goddess of wealth, is traditionally worshipped in the hopes of bringing wealth and happiness to a family or to a business. Tradition also holds that it's an auspicious day to buy precious metals such as gold and silver. After Dhanteras, the next most important Hindu festival for buying gold is Akshaya Tritiya. Like most auspicious days in the calendar, both festivals have deep mythological roots. According to one of several different mythological accounts, Dhanteras is the day when the divine nectar of immortality emerged from the cosmic oceans after it was churned by the gods and the demons. Akshaya Tritiya is associated with the Hindu god Kubera (also known as Karthikeya), considered the god of wealth—hence the auspiciousness of acquiring gold and jewellery on a day in his honour. What's more Akshaya Tritiya leads into the month of Shraavan, which normally falls in late July up till the third week of August in the Western calendar. This month kicks off an auspicious time for marriages, which is a time when gold and jewellery are in high demand for use in adornment and for giving as gifts such as dowries. As with Dhanteras, the price of gold in the Indian market often spikes on Akshaya Tritiya and tapers off thereafter.

On both Dhanteras and Akshaya Tritiya, in keeping with this old tradition, many people buy precious metals such as gold and silver, but gold in particular has always been a prized metal for Indian families. They buy it in the form of gold bars, coins, jewellery, and more recently, even in electronic form such as 'E-gold', which are certificates redeemable in gold as well as mutual funds and exchange traded funds (ETFs), which invest in gold. So great is the fascination with gold that Indian households own nearly one trillion dollars' worth of it, according to a report published in late 2011 by the Australian investment firm Macquarie. To put that number in context it's equivalent to about 50 per cent of the nominal GDP in a given year and the total stock of gold weighs about 18,000 tonnes or 11 per cent of the world's total. According to estimates almost seven per cent or eight per cent of the total household savings in India are in the form of gold. This could partly be explained by purely economic considerations, such as the fact that especially for many rural households, gold is just about the only form of safe and trustworthy investment available as they don't have ready access to financial institutions or property markets. Also, it's possible that gold is used at least in part as a means to stash black money which obviously can't be put in the bank and declared to tax authorities. But beyond this, cultural factors surely are at work and help explain the large amount of gold Indians own compared to people from other countries.

The beliefs that give rise to a cultural fascination with gold, that at least in part helps explain its attraction to Indian investors, aren't part of the Western cultural tradition, but what's beyond doubt is that it seems to make good business sense to cater to those beliefs whether you happen to share them or not. The Swiss are not known for their belief in Hindu mythology or ritual. Yet the World Gold Council, based in Switzerland, especially targeted Indian consumers in the lead-up to Akshaya Tritiya in 2012, offering generous discounts on Swiss-made gold coins, which would be made available at selected branches of the Indian postal service.

Ajay Mitra, the Indian marketing director for the World Gold Council, was quoted in its press release as saying: 'Gold and gold jewellery bought and worn on this important day signifies never-diminishing good fortune. The traditional and cultural appeal of gold, combined with its strong fundamentals, means the precious metal remains central to Indian households' long-term investment strategies, and never more so than during the festival of Akshaya Tritiya.' What's remarkably clever about this quote is how Mitra combines the traditional Hindu belief in the auspiciousness of buying gold during Akshaya Tritiya with a Western MBA-style appeal to gold's strong fundamentals as part of a long-term investment strategy.

As the Macquarie report itself notes, gold, in fact, has outperformed other equities in the Indian market. In the five years before October 2011, for instance, gold rose in value by more than 25 per cent on average per year when measured in Indian rupees per ounce. By comparison, a one-year bank deposit grew only at 8 per cent, and the BSE Sensex (the principal stock index of the Bombay Stock Exchange) grew on average a little over 6 per cent per year during the same period. The fascination with gold at least seems to be a case where traditional belief and modern finance would point the same way.

II

The Indian gold market seems to marry tradition and modernity, but what about the world's most important stock markets? If any market is 'efficient', and presumably immune from cultural influence, surely it's this one?

The economist Gabriele Lepori of the Copenhagen Business School wanted to find out if the stock market could be affected by widely held beliefs seemingly unconnected with economic fundamentals. Drawing on research from fields as diverse as psychology, sociology, and anthropology, Lepori conjectured that the stock markets would be a perfect place for such a test. Far from being always efficient and 'rational', the stock market mixes the perfect cocktail of circumstances for people to resort to received beliefs and habits, which may be distilled from their traditional cultures. The ingredients of this cocktail are that the stakes are high, there's a great deal of uncertainty, and participants feel that they don't have much control over the outcome. Apart from stock markets, you can see how this combination of circumstances perfectly fits, say, professional sports or high stakes gambling.

It's well known that, for example, celebrity sports personalities wear clothing or charms that they believe bring them good luck. The golfer Tiger Woods, for example, is always known for wearing a red T-shirt on Sunday, the last day of a golf tournament. High stakes gamblers, too, are a superstitious lot. Gamblers playing card games such as blackjack will never enter during the middle of a shuffle but will always wait for a fresh deal, as they believe it's bad luck to enter in the middle. This view is widely held even though there's no statistical difference in your odds of winning or losing a given hand at the beginning of a new deal. While it's true that there's no direct instrumental relationship between wearing red or starting at the beginning of a deal and winning, there could be an indirect or psychological relationship that could validate the belief and make it self-fulfilling. For example, if Tiger Woods feels more confident wearing red and so plays better, he'll be more likely to win. And when he does, the fact that he won wearing red will validate his belief. Sticking with the golf example, a group of psychological researchers from Cologne, Germany, found that test subjects who were told that a golf ball was lucky sank 35 per cent more putts than those told their ball was just regular.

For this sort of thinking to have an impact on globalized stock markets, Lepori had the challenge of finding a traditional belief that fulfilled at least two important conditions. First, it had to be a nearly universally shared belief. For example, a number that the Chinese find inauspicious might be auspicious for another community, so that wouldn't work. Second, it had to be a belief that affected everyone at more or less the same time. If it happened at different times, the effects might not show up in the markets because a 'bad' event in one part of the world might be offset by a 'good' event somewhere else. He found the perfect instance of a belief which passed both of these tests—the almost universal belief in all civilizations that eclipses, either solar or lunar, are inauspicious. Greek and Roman writers, including Aristotle, often described lunar eclipses as prophesying earthquakes or storms. The Roman historian Plutarch claimed that people regarded eclipses as 'monstrous and as a sign sent from God portending some great misfortunes'. In the same spirit, the Christian gospel of Luke observes that a solar eclipse occurred at the time of Jesus's death.

In Hindu mythology, eclipses are seen as an inauspicious occurrence of the demon Rahu 'swallowing' or 'biting' the sun or moon and, therefore, hiding parts of them from the earth. In fact, that's why Rahu is portrayed as a demon's head with no body. According to Hindu mythology, he drank some of the divine nectar that makes the gods immortal. The sun and moon realized it and had an avatar of Vishnu cut off the head before the nectar could pass his throat. The body died but the head remained immortal. It's believed that it is this immortal head occasionally swallowing the sun or the moon out of revenge that causes eclipses. When they pass through the open neck, the eclipse ends.

The other vital feature of eclipses is that they occur at more or less the same time everywhere, at any rate within the span of a few hours, so an eclipse should fall on the same or adjacent trading day in all major markets.

Lepori collected data on 362 solar and lunar eclipses visible anywhere in the world from 1928 to 2008. He then looked at the performance of four American stock market indices, the Dow Jones Industrial Average, the S&P 500, the New York Stock Exchange Composite, and the Dow Jones Composite Average. Using data on these four stock indices, he determined the daily returns for each index and so was able to compare average returns on normal days as against those days which had an eclipse.

Conventional economic theory would predict that an aversion to trading on eclipse days or other such beliefs should have no effect on the markets. In what is commonly called the 'efficient markets hypothesis', the markets are populated by rational calculating agents who always figure out the fundamental worth of a stock or any other asset. Since an eclipse presumably wouldn't affect the fundamental value of a stock, rational investors would ignore it. And even if it did (say, for a company manufacturing visors to watch an eclipse), the dates of eclipses are predictable in advance and so shouldn't affect the market the way a piece of financial news does: it should already be priced in to the value of the stock. What's more, if some 'irrational' investors dumped a stock or didn't buy it because of an aversion to trading on an eclipse day, the rational investor would step in and perform 'arbitrage' (in this case, profiting from buying a stock whose value is artificially low) to benefit from this opportunity.

Amazingly, despite the huge number of traders involved from all over the world who have so much to gain or lose from even minuscule movements in the market, Lepori found a small but definite effect caused by eclipses. In the three days surrounding an eclipse, at least three of the four stock indices showed average returns which were lower than normal, as well as lower than normal trading volumes. This reflected the fact that eclipse-conscious traders were investing less on those dates, which would tend to drive the price of the stock down. The negative effect was small, a fraction of one per cent, but it was very much there. Interestingly, he also found that eclipses had a bigger effect the bigger they were. For example, a total eclipse would have a bigger effect than a partial eclipse. He also found that the stock indices returned to their normal levels in the days following an eclipse, what he called a 'reversal effect', which is nothing other than normal market activity returning stock prices to their fundamental levels.

Even though the average daily effect of eclipses was small, Lepori was able to show that over time these small effects would add up to a hefty sum. Let's put that in perspective. Suppose, hypothetically, you had been able to buy into the Dow Jones Industrial Average in 1928 and were patient and long-lived enough to hang on to it until the end of the study period, 2008, for a total of 80 years. You would have increased your money by 37 times your original investment, which sounds really good. But suppose your clever and market-savvy friend did the same as you, except they sold just before each eclipse and bought back right afterwards. Your friend would have increased their money by a whopping 55 times their original investment! This calculation assumes there were no transaction costs such as brokerage fees. Even with such fees, the second investor would make more than the first, although their gains would be smaller in magnitude.

III

Economists Nicole Fortin, Andrew Hill, and Jeff Huang of the University of British Columbia discovered something peculiar about the Vancouver housing market. Vancouver, a city on the west coast of Canada, is home to many ethnic Chinese residents. The researchers found that remarkably, in Chinese-dominated parts of town (defined as areas with a Chinese population higher than the city-wide average of 18 per cent) houses with street numbers ending in the numeral '4' sold at a 2.2 per cent discount as compared to the rest of the market. By contrast, houses with street numbers ending in the numeral '8' sold at a 2.5 per cent premium compared to the rest of the market.

So what's going on? Fortin and her collaborators explain this with reference to Chinese numerology, in which, the numeral '8' is seen as auspicious because it's phonetically close to the Chinese character denoting prosperity and wealth. On the flip side, the numeral '4' is inauspicious because the way in which that Chinese word is pronounced is similar to the word for death in Mandarin, Cantonese, and other Chinese dialects. This traditional belief affects everything from telephone numbers to licence plates and the preference for floor numbers and street numbers; as a simple example, high-rise buildings catering to the Chinese will often omit floor numbers that include the numeral 4. These include buildings not just in China but several important Las Vegas casinos and many apartment buildings in the city of Vancouver. Perhaps it's no accident that the Summer Olympics in Beijing kicked off at exactly 8 p.m. on the eighth day in the eighth month in year 2008, since this would have been a highly auspicious start date and time in numerological terms. Despite newspaper accounts that the start date of the Olympics might have been picked for its auspicious significance, an American television executive, for one, denied that was the reason saying it was just logistics to accommodate other big sports events. Perhaps the stars were just aligned.

Beliefs and behaviour interact in complex and subtle ways. In the case of Indians' fascination with gold, the link is pretty straightforward: they invest in it, and that effect shows up in the markets. Or, in the case of eclipses, investors seem to hold back on inauspicious days, and stock prices reflect that. Or yet again, Chinese numerology has a directly measurable impact on the Vancouver property market. But, other times, deeply held beliefs aren't manifested directly in the sphere of economics and business, but in some of the most intimate and personal decisions that individuals and families take.

If you look at demographic statistics for Japan during the past century, two years dramatically stand out: 1906 and 1966. The fact that these two years were separated by exactly 60 years gives us an important clue.

Japan uses a modified version of the Chinese zodiac, which in turn is the basis for its traditional calendar. In a 12-year cycle, each year is represented by a creature of some sort, such as the dragon, horse, rooster, etc. Overlaid on the 12-year cycle is a different cycle, one which varies every five years and which associates each year with one of the primary elements that are said to make up the universe, such as earth, fire, water, etc. This means that exactly every 60 years, every element in the zodiac will coincide with each one of the five elements. The year 2012, for instance, is the 'Year of the Water Dragon' and 2013 is the 'Year of the Water Snake'.

As it turns out, both 1906 and 1966 were the 'Year of the Horse'—but it was no ordinary horse. They were also years associated with the element of fire. Thus each of those two years was the 'Year of the Fire Horse', which the Japanese call 'Hinoeuma'.

Both years saw big falls in the country's birth rate, and each was followed by a rise the next year. In 1906, the birth rate dropped by 7 per cent, but then rebounded by 16 per cent the following year. In 1966, the birth rate dropped by an even bigger 25 per cent, and the following year jumped by a massive 42 per cent. What accounts for these dramatic spikes down and up separated by six decades? Was this just a strange coincidence, or is there some relationship between Fire Horse years and years with low birth rates?

According to Japanese tradition, girls born in the year of the Fire Horse will grow up to be aggressive and headstrong women who'll be impossible to 'tame' by their husbands and so will be sure to bring bad luck to the family. Japanese parents who hold this traditional belief would presumably want to avoid giving birth to a daughter in a Fire Horse year, as it would be very difficult for her to marry in a culture in which others shared the same belief. In 1906 prenatal sex determination wasn't available, and even in 1966 it wasn't yet widely available. In other words, even if they wanted to, parents trying to avoid having a daughter didn't have the option of sex-selective abortion. Ruling out the grisly possibility of female infanticide (which almost certainly did occur in both of those years), the only other way to prevent having a daughter in those years would be to avoid having a child altogether.

Demographers believe that the year of the Fire Horse explains the big drop-off in birth rates in 1906 and 1966. It simultaneously also explains why birth rates bounced back in 1907 and 1967: presumably parents who delayed having a child the previous year helped bump up the birth rate the following year. Technology also helps explain why the effect was so much bigger in 1966 than in 1906, when you might have expected the opposite: surely the belief in tradition, even in Japan, was stronger in the earlier than the later year? But the key is that back in 1906, modern abortion techniques weren't available, so families who wanted to be sure to avoid having a baby would either have had to practise abstinence in the lead up to and at least part way through the year or, as we've suggested, commit female infanticide. By contrast, in 1966, even though sex-selection wasn't available, abortion was, making it much easier to avoid having a child.

Such huge swings in birth rates are sure to have big effects. On the upside someone born in the year of the Fire Horse will be part of a smaller cohort and, therefore, will face less competition for space in everything from day care to university admission to the job market. On the downside, as they grow older, Fire Horse women may find it tough to find a marriage partner and Fire Horse men who hold to the traditional belief may not want to marry a woman from their own birth cohort but will need to marry someone slightly older or younger.

Economist Hideo Akabayashi of Keio University in Japan has looked at the data to see if this is indeed what happened to the Fire Horse kids from 1966. He finds that it did. First, both men and women born in 1966 found it tougher to find marriage partners. Second, the Fire Horse kids were more likely to be a first child and to have attended a Japanese 'national' college, which are top-rung post-secondary institutions. Third and last, he found that women who were only children and went to college were also less likely to get married.

It's hard to fit all of the pieces of this jigsaw puzzle together, but Akabayashi offers a persuasive story that what was going on was that Fire Horse men were choosing not to marry Fire Horse women and thereby diminishing their own matrimonial prospects. On the other hand, some Fire Horse women may have chosen to marry late or even not to marry at all because they got access to high-quality college education as part of a small cohort. Like a medieval morality tale, it seems that the 'discriminators', as Akabayashi terms the Fire Horse men, ended up suffering more than the 'discriminated', the Fire Horse women who ended up becoming better educated.

As we already mentioned, 2012 is the 'Year of the Dragon', which, like every zodiac sign in the Chinese and related calendars, appears once every 12 years. What makes the Dragon special is that it's the only mythical creature in the zodiac, so that Dragon years in the calendar inherit this mythological power: they are considered the most auspicious years for birth, marriage, or business deals.

So if Dragon years are generally auspicious, what would it mean to be born in the 'Year of the Dragon'? According to traditional Chinese belief, which goes back millennia, Dragon kids are thought to be smarter, stronger, luckier, and generally better than the unfortunate non-Dragon kids born in other signs of the zodiac. (Neither of us, alas, is a Dragon kid.)

Before family planning became widely available, it truly was a matter of luck if you were born a Dragon kid or not. But with family planning, parents who believe in the auspiciousness of the year of the Dragon could try to time the birth of their kids and so 'engineer' them as Dragon kids. This is exactly what has happened in many countries with large ethnic Chinese populations as well as other Asian countries such as Vietnam with similar belief systems. For example, in 1976 and again in 1988, both Dragon years, there were big spikes in birth rates in Taiwan, Hong Kong, and Singapore, all of which have large ethnic Chinese populations.

The biggest effect was in Taiwan where in 1976 the birth rate jumped a whopping 15.5 per cent compared to the previous year. This got the authorities worried. In 1987, the year before the next Dragon year, they issued warnings to alert parents to the problems that Dragon kids would face, such as being born into a very large cohort, being in crowded classrooms, and competing for scarce jobs when they became adults. They were hoping to prevent another surge in births the following year. But the power of traditional belief, it seems, turned out to be stronger than dire government warnings: the birth rate spiked again in 1988 by 7.6 per cent. Interestingly enough, these kinds of spikes haven't as yet been recorded in mainland China itself, perhaps because of the draconian one child policy, so that parents were grateful to have at least one child no matter when he or she was born. It's also possible that official Communist propaganda, which tried to suppress traditional beliefs, might have had some influence.

Economists Noel Johnson and John Nye of George Mason University wanted to study the Dragon kids, but do so in a context with reliable data and where they could compare people who hold Chinese traditional beliefs with people who don't. The perfect test case was the US, which has a large Asian population. They gathered data on Asian Americans, including recent immigrants, to see if they could trace Dragon year effects. They found that Asian Americans who are Dragon kids have about a third of a year more education on average than non-Dragon Asian kids. When they looked at just new immigrants, this education advantage increased to about half a year.

So what did Johnson and Nye discover? In their own words: 'Asian American dragons experience good fortune because they have good parents.' What they mean by this is that Asian mothers of Dragon kids from 1988 or 2000 are more educated, wealthier, and older than non-Asian mothers of kids who just happened to be born in a Dragon year. This is especially pronounced for mothers who only had one child.

More educated and wealthier parents who are better able to time their children's birth than poorer and less educated parents are 'selecting' their kids into Dragonhood. The surprising implication is that, like any powerful belief, the Dragon year is self-fulfilling, much like Tiger Woods wearing red on Sundays. In other words, because the parents of the 1988 and 2000 Dragon kids believed it and those who were richer and more educated were better able to act, they'll likely raise kids who'll do better than average and thereby reinforce a precedent for future generations of parents who will perfectly rationally see that Dragon kids are doing better than non-Dragon kids and will themselves try to keep the pattern going. Of course, as Johnson and Nye themselves point out, this doesn't mean that a preference for Dragon kids will continue in perpetuity. It's possible, for example, that seeing the success of Dragon kids, other parents, too, as they get richer might try to time their kids' birth so as to make them Dragon kids. And if enough parents do this, the Dragon cohort will get overcrowded and not as attractive to be in.

It should be evident by now that traditional beliefs remain important even in a modern economy. Higher birth rates, for instance, feed into businesses that cater to the needs of kids. And there's evidence that such businesses in places with large ethnic Chinese populations thrive in Dragon years. That seems to be holding true, at least as far as we can judge in the middle of 2012 when we're writing this. One news story reported that assisted reproduction clinics in the US, China, and other countries experienced a jump in demand in the lead up to the year of the Dragon. One particular Los Angeles-based surrogacy agency saw a 250 per cent increase in their business from Chinese or Chinese-American clients in the lead up to the 2012 Dragon year. Another news story documented the big increase in early childhood health care expenditures in Hong Kong associated with the year of the Dragon. The Hong Kong government itself anticipates a 5 per cent spike in births in 2012, although independent experts think it might be as high as 10 per cent. When all is said and done, we'll know if there will yet again be a spike in the birth rate and another large cohort of Dragon kids entering the world.

IV

Devdutt Pattanaik isn't your typical business management guru. He's a medical doctor by training, not an MBA. And rather than spewing Harvard Business School case studies, his approach to management issues is decidedly unconventional. When we caught up with him in Mumbai, we were interested in understanding his very unusual job description. When he's not lecturing, consulting, or writing based on his unique perspective on management issues, he serves as 'Chief Belief Officer' for Future Group. The company, headed by entrepreneur Kishore Biyani, is one of India's biggest and most important business conglomerates. Among other things the ubiquitous Big Bazaar, a chain of department stores all over India, anchors their retail business.

So what's a Chief Belief Officer? Is he supposed to impart or validate the beliefs of the company's employees? Far from it. As Devdutt describes it, his mission is to get people to question their beliefs from the ground up and then use the insight they gain to rethink their goals, objectives and even their purpose in life and in business. What makes him unique is that he accomplishes this not through psychoanalysis, as you might have expected given his medical background, but from investigating the foundation of beliefs themselves. In Devdutt's world view, mythology is central. This might seem strange from a Western point of view where mythology is understood rather narrowly as a set of traditional beliefs often associated with religion and generally seen as irrational or at best non-rational in our modern scientific world. The Greek word 'mythos', after all, refers to a story, so mythology on this view is basically a collection of stories.

Devdutt refutes this narrow vision. He defines a myth as 'subjective truth'. Any belief which someone subjectively holds potentially classifies as a myth. Equally, he critiques the standard Western assumption that scientific knowledge is rational and all other traditional knowledge, including mythological, is non-rational. As he sees the world, all beliefs are fundamentally irrational at their root. It's just that the Western scientific view of the world has become so dominant, or 'hegemonic' in the jargon used by cultural theorists, that everyone assumes by default that this is the only correct way to view the world and all other ways must be inferior and irrational. Devdutt turns this idea on its head and argues that the apparently secular capitalism of the West in fact is a thinly veiled descendent of the Greco-Roman and Judeo-Christian mythological traditions that have dominated Western civilization.

While this is a controversial hypothesis, the close relationship between economic and political ideologies on the one hand and religion on the other shouldn't be. After all, it was Max Weber, the founder of modern sociology, who famously theorized that capitalism could arise in northern Europe because of the spirit of thrift and discipline embodied in the Protestant work ethic. Devdutt in a sense is taking Weber head on by suggesting, to the contrary, that capitalism really is only a disguised version of Protestant Christianity and not a logical outgrowth of it.

These ideas are not as bizarre or far-fetched as they might seem. Mircea Eliade was one of the great scholars of religion and mythology of the twentieth century. Originally from Romania, and after many wanderings through Europe, India and beyond, he ended his career as a distinguished professor at the University of Chicago. In some of his writings, Eliade argued that modern ideologies such as capitalism or Marxism are nothing other than 'secularized mythology'. Memorably, he described the Marxist belief in the victory of the proletariat over the bourgeoisie as accomplished through revolution to be 'a truly Messianic Judeo-Christian ideology'. Jesus Christ and Karl Marx aren't so far apart, after all.

Such a heterodox approach questions the often unspoken idea that there's one 'right' way to run a modern business, which is according to textbook Western management theories as taught in business schools. Such theories would hold, say, that a business, if it is to attract investors, must have a 'vision statement', of the type that would be provided by hiring a well-known management consulting firm. As Devdutt argues, most home-grown Indian businesses don't follow a Western-style business plan. Rather, they operate as they have for generations, in a manner that seems well-suited to their particular environment but which may not necessarily make sense elsewhere. But this home-grown approach by no means prevents them from turning a tidy profit.

Likewise, conventional management theory would hold that a large company must have a well-defined organizational hierarchy with precise designations such as chief executive officer, chief operating officer, etc. And indeed large publicly traded corporations do have such conventional hierarchies. But the majority of Indian businesses aren't traded on the stock exchange; most small and medium-sized businesses, and even some larger ones, are privately held and are run by their founding families with organizational hierarchies that are amorphous at best. Devdutt's own designation at Future Group is perhaps a cheeky allusion to this.

Mythology for Devdutt serves the role of helping to clarify people's thinking and get back to basics. He resists the notion that his is a uniquely Indian or even Hindu approach to business management. Rather, he claims that he draws on the relevant mythological tradition based on whomever he's advising or speaking to. So, since most of his work is in India he tends to draw on Hindu and related mythology, but if he were in the US for example, he would draw on Judeo-Christian or Greco-Roman mythology as appropriate.

Here's an example of his method at work. According to classical economic theory and business management models as well, the mission of a business should be to maximize its profits (economics) or shareholder value (business management). What would be the effects of a model based solely on the profit motive? In Hindu mythology, Lakshmi is the goddess of wealth and is an object of worship. But she's never worshipped in isolation, but instead, along with other members of the Hindu pantheon such as, for example, her consort Vishnu, the god who regulates and preserves the universe. What's the lesson? That the pursuit of profit is fine, but if it becomes single-minded and to the exclusion of all other objectives, you're likely to get into trouble.

If this sounds like a radical perspective, think again. Observers from Wall Street, the US Treasury Department, and the International Monetary Fund, bastions of the established order of global capitalism, themselves will concede that the recent global financial crisis clearly points to the failures of poorly regulated financial markets and unfettered global capital flows, in which banks made loans they never should have and poor Americans took out mortgages they couldn't afford. Greater prudence on the part of both borrowers and lenders might have prevented such a crisis. The same could be said for the Euro crisis unfolding in 2012 at the time we write this, precipitated by German and other Western banks lending money to governments like Greece, which the banks knew they'd never be in a position to repay and those governments accepting the money also knowing the same thing.

Conventional economics would suggest that the missing element in these financial crises was the appropriate prophylactic government regulation, and that is certainly a view we would endorse. But this myth-based perspective offers a complementary view. One such as Devdutt might ask, perhaps the real root of the crisis was the unbridled desire for profit that would make stringent regulation necessary in the first place? Whether you agree or not, it's certainly true, at the very least, that individual prudence and government regulation are complements, if not substitutes: a dose of each might have helped prevent the crisis, or perhaps attenuate it. Interestingly, both India and China averted a financial crisis and were spared the worst of the global downturn in the first instance because they didn't take the orthodox advice and didn't completely open up their financial markets.

One interpretation is that the Indians and Chinese were simply better economists than the folks in New York or Washington! But another interpretation would be that cultural traits in both countries led them to adopt a more prudent approach to opening up their markets rather than embracing the free-for-all ethos of Anglo-American capitalism. By the same token, the Russians too, have followed a different path of economic and political development, not necessarily to the liking of the West (or indeed of their own liberals). The so-called 'Washington consensus', if it ever existed, has now been replaced by sets of different, country-specific policies, followed in the major emerging economies, from India and China to Brazil, Russia, and South Africa. Again, we're not suggesting that the conventional economic perspectives on globalization are necessarily wrong; far from it. We suggest merely that supplementing these with a culturally sensitive gaze gives greater depth and nuance to our understanding of why things happen the way they do in different places.

Sometimes, all that's needed in interpreting the difference

between how things happen in the West and how they happen in India is a dose of common sense.

Take charity. A much quoted study by Bain & Co., the American consulting firm, found that private charitable giving in India was just 0.3–0.4 per cent of GDP. (Bain & Co.'s been in the news at the time of writing this in 2012 thanks to its association with Republican Presidential candidate Mitt Romney, who, with his partners, founded Bain Capital. Ironically enough, there's an Indian connection here since President Obama had alleged that during Romney's tenure at Bain, he gave advice that led jobs to be outsourced to India.) By comparison the comparable figure for the US was 2.2 per cent in 2009 and in the UK it was 1.3 per cent in 2010, all according to Bain. Some of this discrepancy can certainly be explained by simple economics. A third of the population of India lives below the poverty line and another third, the middle class, don't have high disposable incomes by Western standards. It's really only the top third of the pyramid who would have enough money to become charitable donors in any big way, and then only really the high net worth individuals at the very top. So it makes sense that charitable giving as a share of the country's national income in India is lower than it would be in the US or UK, where even middle class families make enough money that they can and frequently do give something to charity.

It could also be that Indians are more reluctant to give to charities because they're worried that the money they give might not actually get to the people it's supposed to help. Take Oxfam India, a branch of the respected UK-based charity Oxfam. In their 2011–12 annual report, they disclosed that they devoted about 8 per cent of their total expenditure to fundraising alone. And fundraising expenditures in the range of 8–12 per cent are well within the norm for major charities. If you add in overhead expenditure, then a big chunk, maybe even a third or more, of donations get eaten up in non-programmatic expenses. Since categories of expenditure might be fungible, there's really no way to be sure how much money a given charity is spending on overhead and how much on its programmes. As an example, money spent on TV advertisements or flyers could be classified as educational or equally, they could be classified as fundraising. And of course this is true not just of charities in India but elsewhere too. Yet another theory would hold that there's less charity in India because the country is so ethnically and religiously diverse. In a diverse society, money given to a large public charity such as Oxfam is likely to benefit not just your own ethnic or religious group, but might spill over to others as well, so you might be less likely or less willing to give. While there's no study of this idea for India, a US study using Canadian data does find exactly this.

These conventional economic explanations are surely important. But another part of the story, that tends to get short shrift, lies in understanding the cultural differences in the way that charity works in India compared to Western countries. For example, devout Hindus are inclined to give money or gifts to their preferred religious institution, such as a temple. Devout Vaishnavites, for instance, followers of the Vishnu sect of Hinduism, will give to temples such as Sri Padmanabhaswamy temple in Thiruvananthapuram, or the

Shrinathji temple in Rajasthan, and likewise for the other major Hindu sects (Shaivite, Mother Goddess).

Likewise, devotees of individual gurus or godmen will often give directly to that individual. The most famous recent example is the late Sathya Sai Baba: at the time of his death, the value of the trust he owned and ran was estimated at about $9 billion. That's a huge sum by any standard and shows the power of faith, and of giving, in India. The point is that such religious giving often doesn't show up in the kind of official measurements of charity that Bain & Co. came up with applying their boilerplate Western model. Few temples and certainly no godmen that we've heard of give charitable receipts when plied with money, ornaments, or gold by their devotees. Yet, this *is* charitable giving and it's being entirely missed out by the conventional measurement that only looks at official donations to registered charities backed up by a tax receipt.

On the other hand, even conventional Western-style charities may be able to enhance the donations they do receive by providing an explicitly religious (or cultural) motivation. Here's a personal example that arose by sheer coincidence, as we were writing this chapter—we were buying tickets on-line from the budget Indian airline Indigo. Towards the end of our purchase, the screen menu prompted us to add ten rupees to support a charity which helps children. Normally, being good economists, we'd bypass such a request, but here it was billed as 'good karma', and we instinctively clicked 'yes'.

Quite apart from religiously motivated giving, many Indian families also give generously in ways that don't show up in official statistics and, therefore, is not officially considered 'charity'. To take an everyday example, Indians will routinely come to the help of the families of their domestic staff, often going so far as to pay medical or educational expenses of children or other relatives. Then there are people who give in kind, such as donating medicines to a local hospital to help poor patients who can't afford to buy their own, or restaurants who'll make sure that food uneaten at the end of the night will feed hungry people. All of these forms of generosity would go unrecorded and Indians would be deemed unfairly to be less charitable than they truly are.

Of course, it's a fair point that these more unofficial forms of giving might be less 'efficient' than organized Western-style charity. And as we saw with the Sri Padmanabhaswamy temple, huge amounts of wealth might be lying in sealed vaults and, therefore, not used for productive investment. You could argue it would be like someone keeping money under their mattress rather than putting it into the bank, where it could be subsequently lent out to a borrower and so enter the financial system. While theoretically valid, this criticism misses altogether the cultural context of religious giving. Devotees who give generously to a temple do so out of their religious faith, and not because they're expecting the temple to go and put the money in the bank. Rather, they would expect that the money they and other devotees give would be used to maintain the temple, clothe and feed the people who live and work there, and perhaps support local temple-run organizations such as a school or a hospital. And they would fully expect the temple to accumulate wealth within its walls rather than through conventional investments.

A temple likewise wouldn't contemplate liquidating individual pieces of gold or jewellery and certainly not religious icons that they've been given by patrons and donors. It's said that one small solid gold icon of Vishnu, encrusted with gems, and found in vault 'A' of the Sri Padmanabhaswamy temple, is worth $30 million. Is that like money under the mattress? To the non-religious it might be. But for a temple to sell, or worse still melt down, a priceless icon such as this would be sacrilegious and simply not something they'd contemplate. In more technical terms, these precious gifts have not been 'commodified': they have an intrinsic value to those who possess them where the question of attaching a monetary value simply doesn't arise. Surely, such sentiments must be respected, and certain things considered off limits in the world of business and commerce: much like slavery and child labour now are throughout the civilized world.

Whether it's devotees giving to temples, the impact of eclipses on the stock market, or families planning the birth of their kids around lucky years, there's a common thread: the economic importance of subjective, and often culturally specific, systems of belief, often emanating from history, religion, and mythology. Such belief systems may or may not be 'rational' or 'desirable' from any one particular culture's point of view, but they're there and they do have an effect on economic, social, and even historical outcomes.

V
POSTSCRIPT: THE BIRTH OF THE INDIAN NATION

Perhaps it's fitting that events surrounding the birth of India as a postcolonial nation-state were themselves importantly affected by a traditional belief—in this case, astrology. Shortly before midnight, late on August 14, 1947, the Constituent Assembly of British India convened for the last time in an extraordinary midnight session. The occasion was no less than the end of two centuries of colonial rule and the birth of independent India. 'At the stroke of the midnight hour', in Nehru's famous phrase, the new nation was born.

But why midnight?

In the months leading to independence and the Partition of undivided India into the successor states of India and Pakistan, India's last Viceroy, Lord Mountbatten, had picked the date of August 15 for independence. The plan was for him to fly to Karachi on August 14 to hand over power to Mohammad Ali Jinnah as the first Governor-General of Pakistan. He would return to Delhi that night and the birth of India was to be proclaimed on the morning of August 15. But there was a problem. It turned out that just weeks before independence Mountbatten had been told that astrologers deemed August 15 an inauspicious day.

As recounted by Dominique La Pierre and Larry Collins in *Freedom at Midnight*, on August 15, India would fall under the zodiac sign known in India as Makara, or the Capricorn, which was thought hostile to 'centrifugal forces' and hence to the Partition of India. Even worse, that day would fall under the influence of Saturn, an inauspicious planet, and dominated by Rahu, whom we've already encountered as the demon that traditionally is believed to cause eclipses. Astrologically it would have been tough to pick a worse day for independence. One swamy wrote to Mountbatten and told him: 'For the love of God, do not give India her independence on 15 August. If floods, drought, famine and massacres follow it will be because free India was born on a day cursed by the stars.'

Since the creation of Pakistan was already fixed for August 14 what could be done? Any delay could prove catastrophic in the atmosphere of Hindu–Muslim acrimony and suspicion in the dying days of the British Raj. The economic, to say nothing of the political, cost of a delayed Indian independence would be impossible to calculate. A solution had to be found and quickly. In a speech given many years later, Mountbatten credits Nehru for coming up with an 'ingenious' solution to what he saw as a 'ludicrous' problem. (Some contemporary sources credit the civil servant K.M. Panikkar as the author of this ingenious solution.) To placate the gods but keep independence on track, the Constituent Assembly would meet a little before midnight so that India's independence could still be proclaimed when it was technically August 14, with Nehru's 'tryst with destiny' speech beginning just after the chimes of midnight. This way history would record August 15 as India's Independence Day, as it's been celebrated every year since.

Myth and modernity are, it would seem, inseparable in India.

6

News from India

I

The National Intelligence Council (NIC) is a think tank within the US government that provides intelligence to the President and his or her security establishment. While the Central Intelligence Agency (CIA) sends James Bond-like operatives out into the field to protect America's national security, the NIC issues periodic reports on matters that could indirectly affect American national interests. Back in September 2002, they published a report that suggested the prevalence of HIV/AIDS infection in India would rise to a staggering 20–25 million people by the year 2010. The report was immediately endorsed by the world's richest man, Bill Gates. His charitable foundation, the Bill and Melinda Gates Foundation, pledged $100 million to fight AIDS in India, the largest single donation of that type up to that point in time. Gates was due to meet India's then prime minister, Atal Bihari Vajpayee, to announce the donation and discuss combatting AIDS in India. Despite accepting the donation, not everyone in the government was happy. India's health minister at the time, the former actor Shatrugan Sinha, accused Gates and then American ambassador Robert Blackwill of 'spreading panic' by endorsing what in his view was an overly alarmist prediction.

Still, as far as leaders of the world community were concerned, India was staring disaster in the face. Adding his voice to that of Bill Gates, former US President, Bill Clinton said that India would be the 'epicentre' of the global AIDS epidemic, overtaking sub-Saharan Africa. The endorsement by the two Bills was a shot in the arm for AIDS activists, who'd long felt that Indian officials were understating the true importance of the spread of HIV in India. Rather like an endorsement from Oprah Winfrey, who can sell millions of copies of a book by simply mentioning it in her book club, the support thrown behind the cause of combating AIDS by celebrities such as Gates and Clinton helped focus the attention not only of activists but of the news media as well.

The 2002 announcement, in fact, capped a period of growing concern about HIV/AIDS, both worldwide and in India specifically, running from about the early 1990s to the mid 2000s. Here's a smattering of news headlines from that period, culled more or less at random from domestic and international newspapers: 'India may face AIDS epidemic' (*Times of India*, 1991); 'India seen as ground zero in spread of AIDS to Asia' (*Washington Post*, 1995); 'Denial and taboo blinding India to the horror of its AIDS scourge' (*New York Times*, 1996); 'India cannot afford to wait in the face of AIDS epidemic' (*Times of India*, 1998); 'India appears headed for a public health disaster' (*St. Louis Dispatch*, 2003); 'Global Fund to warn India of impending AIDS catastrophe' (Indo-Asian News Service printed in the *Hindustan Times*, 2005); 'In India, sex trade fuels HIV's spread; women trapped as male-dominated economy booms' (*USA Today*, 2005); and finally, 'AIDS study warns of impact on India's economy' (*New York Times/International Herald Tribune*, 2006). Data from Google Trends also confirms a rising trend in the coverage of stories related to HIV/AIDS through the 1990s and in the case of India, peaking in 2004 and 2005. This makes sense as this was about the peak of the news headlines claiming that India was in the midst of a crisis. Anyone reading the news, or who'd heard about the Gates donation, couldn't have been blamed for thinking that India was on the verge of an AIDS epidemic if not already in the middle of one.

Just as the news coverage was rising to a fever pitch, a group of Indian medical scholars published a paper in a British public health journal. The team, led by Lalit Dandona, a researcher based in Hyderabad at that time, asked whether the burden of HIV/AIDS was being overestimated in India. Their hunch was that the official United Nations methodology that was being used in India as elsewhere was likely to inflate the number of people afflicted with the HIV virus. The reason for this suspicion is that the official methodology extrapolates the burden of HIV by looking at what is called 'sentinel surveillance data' (a system in which a pre-selected sample of reporting institutions provide data on one or more medical conditions as identified in the research plan)—from the antenatal clinics at large public sector hospitals and clinics which treat sexually transmitted infections (STIs). They reasoned that this was likely to cause a bias because the kinds of people who would be using these facilities (such as poor sex workers) would be more likely to be HIV-positive than the population at large. These would also include lower income people who didn't have access to private care and so would have little choice but to seek treatment or diagnosis at public hospitals and STI clinics. To test their hunch, Dandona and his team decided to use intravenous blood tests on people in the Guntur district of Andhra Pradesh and used the results on the number of people actually infected to make inferences about the country as a whole. They picked this district because of the high prevalence of HIV. In a sense, they wanted to stack the deck against themselves. If they found that there were fewer cases of people actually infected in a high prevalence area, this would be a sign that the official statistics were likely overestimating the problem nationwide.

It turned out that the sceptics were right after all.

The explosive results of the Dandona study were a shock for the true believers in the impending epidemic. Rather than the official estimate of 5.2 million people, which would put India at least on the cusp of a serious health crisis, they suggested that fully a third less people, or about 3.5 million, were actually at risk. This number isn't trivial, but in a country of a billion people or more, is not the start of an epidemic. Equally importantly, the people most at risk were in well-known high-risk groups such as sex workers and their customers, people with multiple sexual partners, intravenous drug users, gay men, and long-distance truck drivers. There was little evidence of an epidemic spreading among the mainstream population and away from these high-risk groups. As you might expect, given the climate at that time, these results were widely reported. As you would also expect, they were initially greeted with a great deal of scepticism by those who had a stake in the orthodox measurement, most notably the UN and assorted AIDS activists in India and abroad.

The Dandona study appeared in December 2006. With similar studies in other parts of the world coming to similar conclusions, by November 2007, less than a year later, the UN's official AIDS fighting agency, known as UNAIDS, acknowledged in a report that it had overestimated the number of people worldwide who were suffering from HIV. They further acknowledged that new infections had been steadily dropping year after year since they peaked in the late 1990s. They revised down their estimate of the worldwide infection rate from almost 40 million to a little over 33 million. The revised Indian data came in at 2.5 million, even lower than Dandona's estimate, or about half of the previous official estimate.

So what does this tell us? The obvious lesson is that we all might want to be a bit more cautious when confronting scientific studies that make strong claims about things like the number of people suffering from AIDS. Caution is especially called for if such studies aren't based on direct measurement but extrapolate from a small sample of people using some sort of a statistical model. The Achilles' heel of the UN's method was that they were sampling people at high risk, and further, their statistical extrapolations magnified this even further and gave numbers that were totally out of whack. Remember we told you about the big BJP victory in the 2004 election that didn't happen but was confidently predicted by opinion polls? Exactly the same statistical failure was at work there: oversampling a non-representative population. The UN scientists who came up with their method, of course, only had the best of intentions. They were trying to come up with a reliable estimate of the number of people with AIDS in any given country or worldwide on the assumption, usually correct, that very limited data would be available in each given country. But for better or worse, their method tended to inflate the number of people afflicted, and these inflated numbers the official studies came up with fuelled a climate of hysteria in which pronouncements of an impending epidemic became commonplace and everyone jumped on the bandwagon. Indeed, following the downward revision of the UN statistics, a number of AIDS advocates expressed the fear that support for their cause would drop if not evaporate if the public felt that the threat from AIDS was overblown.

So what of the NIC's much-vaunted prediction that there would be 20–25 million people suffering from HIV/AIDS in India by 2010? The most recent independently verified and reliable estimates we have for the actual infection rate, again reported in another British medical journal, suggest that it was about 1.4–1.6 million in 2004–06, even lower than the already downward revised estimate of 2.3 million for 2006. We don't have a similar independent study as yet for 2010 or beyond, but official Indian government statistics for 2010–11 estimate it at 2.39 million. It's likely that an independent evaluation may well revise this number downward in future.

To be fair, part of the drop in the prevalence of AIDS in India does reflect greater awareness and greater public spending on prevention and treatment. But these interventions cannot explain why the NIC's prediction was so totally out of the ballpark. Rather it's just that those official estimates and predictions were just plain wrong. At least in the case of the HIV/AIDS statistics, the work of Dandona and others has led to a revised methodology with more realistic numbers. But this might be just the tip of the iceberg in the realm of correcting misleading or uninformative data based on problematic methodologies.

Recall Bill Clinton said India would overtake sub-Saharan Africa as the epicentre of the global AIDS epidemic? If you believe claims that were made in early 2012, India also leads sub-Saharan Africa when it comes to child malnutrition. Several Indian and international news organizations ran headlines to the effect that India has twice the number of underweight children as sub-Saharan Africa. These headlines in turn are backed up by statistical research done by international organizations and NGOs interested in children's welfare, again much like how the AIDS data is put together. And once again there's a widely accepted scientific methodology that's used to construct the malnutrition statistics. This methodology hangs on one critical assumption. That assumption is the World Health Organization's (WHO) norm for measuring child malnutrition, which is called the 'Child Growth Standard'. This in turn is based on a sample or 'reference population' which comprises 8,440 healthy young children from the age of 0–60 months. These children come from Brazil, Ghana, Oman, Norway, India, and the US. The theory that lies behind the index is the notion that children should be able to grow equally well with an equivalent amount of nourishment no matter where they're born and importantly, without regard to genetics or ethnicity. In other words a well-fed Indian kid should be about the same height and weight as a well-fed kid of the same age from these other countries.

Next, the WHO's methodology makes the assumption that the bottom 2.14 per cent of the reference group is malnourished or stunted and that the remaining 97.86 per cent are normal and not malnourished. The problem is not with the 2.14 per cent cut-off. That just comes from the usual assumption in statistics that a large enough and 'well-behaved' population can be described by the 'normal' distribution, sometimes also known as the 'bell curve'. In a normal distribution, 2.14 per cent represents two standard deviations below the mid-point and is a perfectly reasonable and defensible cut-off. So where's the problem?

Thinking about the malnutrition statistics, noted Indian economist Arvind Panagariya figured something must be amiss. He's a professor of international affairs at Columbia University and holds a chair in Indian political economy named in honour of Jagdish Bhagwati, the great international trade economist who's often given credit for coming up with the ideas and the intellectual rationale for India's economic reforms starting in 1991.

Panagariya noted that the child malnutrition statistics seemed to be completely at odds with the other relevant socio-economic indicators when you compare India and sub-Saharan Africa. Panagariya explored some of these ideas in an op-ed in the *Times of India* and shared his as yet unpublished research with us. As he explained it to us, there's a huge gap between the percentage of underweight children in India (43 per cent) as in sub-Saharan Africa (25 per cent). That's the basis for the claim that matters are worse in India than in sub-Saharan Africa. But now look at life expectancy: in sub-Saharan Africa it's 54.4 years, while in India it's 65.4, both according to the UN's 2011 Human Development Report. So Indians live on average more than a decade longer than sub-Saharan Africans. Other socio-economic indicators also generally show India doing better than sub-Saharan Africa. Since economic liberalization in 1991, India has seen steady economic growth and no major international conflicts. Sub-Saharan Africa by contrast is a region that is still the world's poorest, has seen many wars and civil wars, much famine and disease, and every manner of economic, social, and political problem. And as we saw earlier it's also been a hotbed of the HIV/AIDS epidemic. When almost all of the statistics suggest that India's doing better than sub-Saharan Africa, which accords with common sense, and there's one statistic going the other way, you have to look closely at that one errant statistic.

Panagariya's theory is that the problem lies with the reference population. He suggests that 'at any given age sub-Saharan African children and those defining the WHO reference population are on average genetically taller and weigh more than Indian children'. What that means is that an Indian child who's in fact healthy but just naturally smaller than the reference group would wrongly be classified as malnourished or stunted. As he wryly notes, even most rich Indian kids would be reckoned malnourished or stunted according to the official measurement. Clearly, something here doesn't add up. Panagariya also told us that he believes similar measurement errors might contaminate adult malnutrition statistics, but the research to back up that claim doesn't yet exist.

Both the AIDS story and the child malnutrition saga generated screaming headlines both in the international and Indian press. That's something they share in common with the hysteria in 2009 over influenza. You'd have hoped that the world might have learned a lesson in the years in between. But it seems that was too much to hope for. In February 2009, a number of influenza cases were discovered in hospitals in Mexico City and the surrounding area. Subsequent tests carried out in the US and Canada revealed that a new strain of the H1N1 influenza virus had hit the scene. It was given the unappetizing name of 'swine flu' since pigs had been the original source of the infection. Within weeks, panic spread, and by June the WHO had declared a worldwide 'pandemic emergency'. But a year later, it became clear that there had been no emergency. In the 2009–10 flu season, roughly 18,000 people had died due to the disease around the world, fewer than in previous seasons, and then many of them were also suffering from more serious underlying medical conditions, and the flu in effect just tipped them over the edge.

So who benefited from what turned out to be a falsely declared flu emergency? The answer: the pharmaceutical companies that made the vaccines to fight the flu. Up to $10 billion was spent around the world to prepare for the flu season, including over $4 billion by the US alone. By March 2010, questions were being raised. A report by the Council of Europe, an international organization headquartered in Strasbourg (not to be confused with the European Union in Brussels), argued that the H1N1 virus was known *not* to be a crisis before the WHO declared it a pandemic. They further expressed concern about the undue influence of big pharmaceutical companies on the activities of the WHO, which is an international organization and part of the UN system—in theory at least independent of private sector influence. While it's never been proved that it was the influence of drug companies that led to the phony flu pandemic, you can draw your own conclusions.

This time though Indians' natural scepticism (you might call it cynicism) meant that there was little more than a token response. We remember flying into Mumbai late in 2009 and just having to tick an extra form saying we didn't have a high fever and an Indian health official dutifully waved us through and said 'welcome home'.

The moral of both the AIDS and child malnutrition stories is the same: when the numbers don't add up, look hard at the statistics and how they were measured before giving up on your common sense.

II

About every two to three seconds, a violent crime against a woman takes place in India. That's according to government statistics. In 2011, the total number of crimes against women was 228,650. That's a little more than a 7 per cent increase from the previous year and close to a 40 per cent increase if you look back to 2005. Since the population is growing somewhere between 1 to 2 per cent per year, these statistics seem to be suggesting that violence against women is increasing. But how do crimes against women in India compare with other countries? What countries are the best and worst for women?

It's intrinsically difficult to compare statistics from one country to another for a variety of reasons. For one thing, different countries measure violence against women in different ways. Some, like Canada for instance, collect data on spousal violence, but this is just one component of violence against women. For another, it's not clear how meaningful it would be to compare statistics between countries that have such different socio-economic conditions. India, for example, is densely populated, whereas Canada and Scandinavian countries are very thinly populated. Something as basic as population density is likely to affect the intensity of violence: when people are cooped together in close quarters, there's more likely to be a spark that incites violence than if people are living miles apart from each other.

Nevertheless, UN Women, the UN agency devoted to gender equity and women's issues, has tried to collect comparable data on what is termed 'intimate partner violence'. This is defined as physical or sexual assault against women carried out by their spouse or by someone with whom they're intimate. According to the UN's data, as of March 2011, in India, almost 24 per cent of women had reported either physical and/or sexual abuse within the last 12 months and 37 per cent reported such abuse some time during their lives. (We should note that these data do not come from government statistics but rather from independent research that the UN agency chose to report.) Compare this to a country like Canada, where the comparable statistics are 2 per cent and 7 per cent respectively. The Indian numbers are high but by no means the highest in the world. Ethiopia, for example, reports the staggeringly high numbers of 54 per cent and 71 per cent respectively. The US data for instance shows a big discrepancy from those reporting intimate partner violence in the last 12 months (1.5 per cent) and in their lifetime (almost 25 per cent). It's partly because of the fact that it's difficult to make sense of cross-country data that NGOs and advocacy groups prefer the approach of surveying experts.

One such survey which has received a great deal of media attention is by TrustLaw Women whom we've encountered in a previous chapter. They're a women's rights news and information service run by the Thomson Reuters Foundation, which in turn was set up by the giant newswire and publishing house. In late spring of 2012, TrustLaw Women conducted their latest poll, a 'global perceptions poll' of 370 experts with knowledge on gender issues. The goal was to rank all of the countries in the Group of 20 (G-20) from best to worst, the criteria being how well women fared. As we advised in a previous chapter, the opinion of experts should be taken with a grain of salt especially when packaged in statistics and snazzy-looking tables and charts. Be that as it may, these experts were asked to rank the three best and the three worst countries for women in seven different categories according to their professional judgement. These categories include: workplace opportunities; access to resources; participation in politics; quality of health; freedom from violence; freedom from trafficking and slavery; and an overall category that was meant to sum everything up. As in their previous survey we told you about, each of the countries got a weighted score in all seven categories based on the number of best and worst votes it received. For example, a score of zero would mean a country received as many positive votes as negative votes. A negative score would mean it received more negative than positive votes and so on. Each category was given equal weight and these were used to compile a final score to rank each country. In their final ranking, the countries at and near the top seem to fit common sense. Canada came in first, followed by Germany, the UK and a group of other rich Western economies. What seems strange though are the countries at the bottom of the league table. India's at the very bottom, at number 19, even behind Saudi Arabia, Indonesia, and South Africa. What is more, India is at or near the bottom of all indicators except for political participation where it comes in at number 17 just ahead of China and Saudi Arabia.

This is where that grain of common sense is required. Is it really conceivable that women in India are even worse off than in Saudi Arabia, where they lack basic civil liberties and need a man's permission to do just about anything? When quizzed about these peculiar results on Twitter, a reporter for Reuters who'd written up a story based on the survey findings gave the surprising reply that because women in Saudi Arabia were cloistered but were freer in India, they actually experienced worse outcomes in India than in Saudi Arabia. This sounds a bit like saying that someone falsely imprisoned in a maximum security prison but who's at least well-fed and clothed is better off than someone who's free but struggling to make a living. You have to wonder what was behind the thinking of the experts who assigned these rankings. The trouble is, we have absolutely no way of knowing since a survey-based ranking like this is completely detached from objectively measured statistics. Flawed though they no doubt are, official statistics on violence against women probably paint a more accurate picture than the summation of the expert opinion of people sitting in offices in Washington, London, or anywhere else.

Imagine you wanted to figure out which countries in the world had the highest and lowest GDP growth in the G-20. Would you conduct a survey of experts or would you look at the official GDP statistics? The official numbers might have their problems, but at least they're based on some sort of methodology that can be scrutinized, analysed, critiqued, and even improved. Indeed, this is exactly what we saw in the first section where scientific research helped improve the methodology by which the incidence of HIV was calculated. Imagine if Dr Dandona and his team had queried experts rather than going into the field? Those experts would probably have trotted out the conventional wisdom and we wouldn't have learned anything.

Rankings like the one by TrustLaw Women in our estimation do a disservice to the plight of suffering women in India and elsewhere. Here's why. They distract from the real questions of how we can make the situation better for women in India or Saudi Arabia for that matter and instead, we get bogged down in meaningless debates about who's at the bottom and who's at the top. And furthermore, someone reading the results of such a ranking who themselves haven't encountered violence against women (either as a victim or a witness) is likely to fixate more on the ranking rather than think deeply about the many problems women, in fact, do face.

But let's step back from the survey and look again at the actual data, which is troubling enough. Most disturbingly, how do we explain the sharp year on year rise in the official government of India statistics for violence against women? Is it really true that crime is going up year after year disproportionately targeting women?

Theoretically, that is a possibility. But what is also possible is that there's greater reporting by women of crimes committed against them, and it's this greater reporting that's showing up in the statistics rather than an actual increase in the amount of crime. Apart from a mere increase in reporting, there are subtler factors that could be at work. For example, a crime that went reported as a generic act of violence might now be classified as violence against women. So what could be happening is both increased reporting and a more accurate classification of the types of violence being committed. A recent study by Harvard Business School professor Lakshmi Iyer and her collaborators suggests that this might actually be going on in India and ironically enough, the political empowerment of women may be one factor.

Even in countries like Canada, which as we saw from official statistics is the safest place in the world for women, until very recently at least a lot of crime against women, especially domestic violence didn't necessarily go reported. The stigma attached to reporting oneself as a victim of domestic violence, fear of reprisal, and economic dependence on one's victimizer kept many women silent. It's in the last three or four decades even in rich countries like Canada and the US, in which women have become economically more independent and in which they have alternatives to facing abuse such as women's shelters that there's been greater reporting. Could it be that India, too, has seen an increase in the reporting of crime against women paradoxically not because things have got worse but because they're starting to get better? We leave that open as a possibility, since all the facts aren't yet in. But we're sure that won't stop the experts from sharing their opinions. (Quite apart from the 'experts', voices in the media, too, continue to weigh in, some commenting without scrutinizing the statistics and engaging in the requisite armchair sociology.)

Possibly one reason why there's extensive media coverage of expert surveys on violence against women, or violence in general, is the relative scarcity of good scholarly work on the subject. One notable exception is a 2000 study by economists Jean Drèze and Reetika Khera. They study the murder rate in India, as calculated from government statistics. Since a case of domestic violence or rape often will require the victim to file a report with the police, which as we've noted, may not always happen, they stick to murder because unlike domestic violence or rape, murder is difficult to hide from the authorities.

They note that the murder rate has been on the rise in India from the mid-1950s until the mid-1990s. In 1995, the last year in the study, the murder rate was 41 per million people. We've looked at the government statistics in the period following the study and the murder rate has actually been trending back down. In 2011, the last year for which we have data, it was down to 28. This looks like a welcome development. Those who'd dismiss this improving trend and criticize government statistics by saying that crimes go under-reported are missing the point. Even if it's true, as it almost certainly is, that crimes are systematically under-reported, what reason would you have to think that the under-reporting has got much worse in the last 10 years? When other crime statistics have trended up, but the murder rate has trended down, that's probably good news. Not only is murder more difficult to hide from the authorities, but in an India saturated with media of all kinds, print, television, and social it's hard to believe that the under-reporting of murder would have increased in the last 15 years. In more technical terms systematic under-reporting of crimes would be expected to affect the level, but not the rate of change, of crime reporting. A falling rate of crime is still good news, even in a world in which some crime goes unreported.

Be that as it may, the study by Drèze and Khera only goes up to 1995 and has not been updated since either by them or by any other scholar. It's a great shame because they provide a rich statistical analysis of the correlation between the murder rate across the states of India with a range of socio-economic indicators. Their most important finding is that there's a strong and 'robust' (statistically sound), negative correlation between the murder rate and the female to male ratio in the population. In other words, in places where there are relatively fewer women than men, the murder rate tends to be high, and vice-versa.

But does this mean that an adverse sex ratio is causing more crime? Not necessarily. A fundamental principle of statistics, which many people including professional economists ignore at their peril, is that the correlation between any two variables you're looking at doesn't necessarily mean there's a cause-and-effect relationship. It could well be that an adverse sex ratio means, for example, that there are lots more unmarried angry men roaming around who end up committing more murders. But it could equally be, at least in theory, that living in a more murder-prone region might cause an adverse sex ratio. Parents, for example, might prefer to have more boys rather than girls if they fear that their daughters could be victims of murder or violent crime.

And in the arcane world of statistical regression, there's a third possibility that your two variables are moving together because of some third underlying factor that you've altogether missed. For example, it could be that both a higher murder rate and an adverse sex ratio are the result of a violent patriarchal society. In fact, different scholars have supported versions of all three of these possibilities. Drèze and Khera themselves lean towards the third hypothesis but fully admit that it's tough to draw firm causal connections. Their well-measured conclusion is that 'there's a strong link of some kind between gender relations and criminal violence'. Now that's the sort of subtle and nuanced conclusion that doesn't make it into screaming headlines.

III

On May 18, 2012, Mangte Chungneijang Mary Kom made history. She became the first and so far only Indian woman to qualify in the new category of women's boxing for the Summer Olympics, which debuted in 2012. It was a nail-biting affair, as Mary Kom, as she's usually known, had lost to England's Nicola Adams in the quarter final of the world championships. Under the convoluted qualification rules, Mary's fate rested in Nicola's hands: if she defeated her Russian competitor in the semi-final round, Mary would qualify. That's exactly what happened and India had its first ever berth in Olympic women's boxing.

Mary's is an unlikely and inspirational story. She hails from Manipur in north-eastern India, which is one of the most economically deprived and remote regions of the country, sandwiched as it is between Bangladesh and Burma and connected to the mainland of India by only a narrow land corridor. Added to its isolation and economic backwardness, the region is home to several insurgencies, which often lead to blockades and worsen the economic deprivation.

Mary's parents are landless agricultural workers. With little opportunity at home, she moved on her own to Imphal, the state capital, to try her luck at a career in track and field. For a young woman to move away from home and pursue a career in amateur sports was in itself a courageous decision. India as a country is notorious for its official government agencies doing little to encourage or support its sports men and women (except, of course, for its star cricketers). (Abhinav Bindra is a rifle shooter and India's only Olympic gold medallist in an individual event. Tellingly, one chapter in his memoir is sarcastically titled 'Mr Indian official: Thanks for nothing'.) Mary ended up switching to boxing, and that changed her life. Through sheer hard work, grit, and tenacity, she pulled herself up into the upper echelons of women's boxing, winning five consecutive gold medals at the world championships until she came up short in 2012. If that's not amazing enough, she won the last two of her five world championships after giving birth to twin boys. As things turned out, in August 2012, Mary clinched a bronze medal at the London Olympics. Sadly, a gold eluded her because she was once again beaten by Nicola Adams, this time in the semifinal match. Still, it's been an incredible journey, and there's no reason to think this is the end.

Remarkably, Mary's story was little known in India until she was featured on the cover of the July/August 2012 issue of *Intelligent Life*, the *Economist* magazine's culture and lifestyle supplement, in a long and evocative essay by Indian novelist Rahul Bhattacharya. Even her Olympic qualification received fairly scant attention in the mainstream Indian press.

In the *Times of India*, the highest circulation daily newspaper in the country in any language, the 'prominent' sports stories on May 19, 2012, included coverage of the Indian Premier League (IPL)—which is the professional cricket league—as well as the European Champions League for football. Mary's story appeared in a box on the fourth and last page of sports coverage just before the gossipy society pages. As for the first page, there was a reference in the right-hand banner below the masthead in the same space that told us of a new book reporting on an alleged passionate affair by the former French First Lady, Carla Bruni. The main front page story above the crease was about match fixing, fighting, and alleged molestation in the IPL.

India's highest circulation Hindi-language daily, *Dainik Bhaskar*, which also commands the second highest circulation in any language after the *Times of India*, similarly featured a thumbnail photo of Mary next to the masthead and the actual story occupying a small box on the single page of sports news. Here, too, the big news stories concerned international cricket, the IPL and the success at the Rome Masters (a warm up-event to the French Open) of tennis stars Roger Federer and Maria Sharapova. Mary once again rates a thumbnail picture, smaller than the picture of Nicola Adams who defeated her. And, of course, accompanying the tennis story it's no surprise that there's a large picture of the glamorous Sharapova.

Next, take the *Indian Express*, another premier English-language daily. Here, there isn't even a mention of Mary's news on the front page and the story once again rates a small box, this time in the lower left-hand corner of the sports page. The main sports story features the championship runs of Chelsea and Bayern Munich in the European Champions League.

To round out our look at the national news coverage, there's *Daily News and Analysis (DNA)*, another high circulation English-language daily. Again, there's nothing on the front page. There's a small box carrying the news on the lower right-hand corner of the sports page but with the disparaging headline 'Back door entry to Olympics for Mary'. To add insult to injury, the sports page on May 20, 2012 includes her in a list of 'who's not [hot]', and points out that she failed to win a medal at the world championships.

Mary's story did make headline news in the *Sangai Express*, an English and Manipuri-language daily newspaper in Mary's home state of Manipur. But it was only following the cover story in *Intelligent Life* and in the run up to the Olympics that Mary's remarkable story was featured more prominently by the mainstream Indian press. And just think of the legions of other Indian women and girls who've had to beat the odds just to survive and make their way in the world, whether of sports, business, science, or anything else and have not made it into the news. Yet the media's coverage of stories that relate specifically to women or girls tends to be by and large bad news stories of abandonment, rape, molestation, domestic violence, murder, and the most extreme forms of the abuse of women.

Of course, we're not for one moment suggesting that these things don't happen. They do; and India does remain a difficult place for women in many ways. Our point is rather a more balanced treatment of women's day to day struggles, both positive and negative, would give a fairer picture both to Indians and the outside world of the true state of women in India. Instead, we seem to see op-eds and editorializing news stories, which relate a specific incident to a wider claim about how awful a place India is for women, sometimes even referring to the TrustLaw survey to help clinch their argument.

So why does bad news outweigh good? A facile but unconvincing answer is what's often called 'media sensationalism': publishers and editors want to sell more newspapers or increase their TV ratings, so they feature the lurid and the violent at the expense of the good and the uplifting. But this just pushes the problem back one stage and begs the question: why would bad news sell and good news not? Once again, cognitive psychology, which we've encountered before, comes to the rescue. It tells us that among the panoply of cognitive failures that humans are prone to suffer from, one of them is 'negativity bias'. In simple terms, this just means that people tend to react more to bad news than to good, and this colours our perception of the world. There may even be an evolutionary explanation for this phenomenon. Our early ancestors lived in a dangerous world in which human mortality was high and perils lurked around every corner. In this kind of world, bad news becomes more salient than good news because it helps improve our chances of survival. For example, 10 or 20 'news reports' that a dangerous predator isn't in the neighbourhood are worth a lot less to your survival than paying heed to that one news report that a predator is nearby. Relatedly, as Cass Sunstein, the Harvard Law School professor whom we've encountered in a previous chapter, has argued in an op-ed, cognitive biases imply that people tend to read even balanced news coverage in a skewed way, giving more weight to what confirms their own preconceptions and discounting what supports other points of view. This is likely to reinforce the negativity bias.

A related cognitive bias looks back nostalgically at the past comparing it favourably to the difficulties of the present. We've seen something of this in our discussion of counterfactuals, whereby some people say things like we were better off under the British, when, in fact, if you examine the objective facts, that certainly isn't true for 99.9 per cent of Indians. It might be true for the odd penniless Maharaja looking back fondly on the bygone days of the Raj.

Are things *really* worse for women in India than they were 50, a 100, or 500 years ago?

IV

In 2011, India released its latest Census, according to which just over 1.2 billion people or about 17 per cent of the world's population live in India. This mammoth exercise is undertaken every ten years. In the 2011 edition, it's reported to have cost almost $500 million. Almost 3 million government officials visited households spread across the vast country going to about 7,000 towns and 600,000 villages.

Among the many findings in the Census, the most worrying of all is that India's childhood sex ratio continues to worsen. In 2011, the Census estimates that there were 914 girls for every 1,000 boys from the ages of 0–6. This is even worse than in 2001, when there were 927 girls for every 1,000 boys. More pointedly, this ratio is the worst ever since the country's independence in 1947.

Such skewed sex ratios are hard to reconcile with nature and strongly suggest the presence of selection in favour of boys, either taking the form of sex-selective abortion or even female infanticide. (Aborting female foetuses is sometimes also referred to as female foeticide. We refrain from using this latter term since we don't want to prejudge the morally difficult question of abortion. We prefer the more neutral term, sex-selective abortion.) In nature, with no sex selection, the observed sex ratio is approximately 1,020 males for every 1,000 females. Genetically, in other words, there's a slightly higher probability of a new birth being a male rather than a female. You can interpret this as evolution's way of making up for the fact that boys suffer higher infant mortality than girls, so that the sex ratio should balance out and be back to 1:1 by about the age of six. Most explanations of the badly skewed sex ratio point to the existence of what's called 'son preference'. In patriarchal societies, parents may have a preference for sons over daughters. The reasons are diverse. In Hindu religious tradition, for example, only sons may perform funerary rights. But economics often interacts with religion. The prevalence of dowry, for instance, means that girls may be more 'expensive' than boys for parents to raise and therefore seen as less desirable. Son preference is by no means unique to India, being ubiquitous throughout Asia and beyond. The end result seems to be that women are 'missing'.

The phrase 'missing women' is a term that was first coined by the Nobel Prize-winning Indian economist Amartya Sen, currently a professor at Harvard. In a pair of influential articles in the early 1990s, Sen argued that the ratio of women to men in developing countries such as India and China were too low to be a natural outcome. He converted these skewed sex ratios into an estimate of the number of missing women by making the assumption that the number of women who 'should' be alive would be comparable to the developed world where sex ratios are not skewed and where men and women receive an equal amount of care. He came up with the staggering statistic that more than 100 million women were missing and many of these were in India and China.

It's important to note that any such calculation requires us to make assumptions about the counterfactual scenario, a concept we've previously referred to. Sen's counterfactual is the assumption that the sex ratio should be balanced and he uses that assumption to figure out how many women are missing. Using a different counterfactual would, of course, give different results. But the bottom line is that any sensible counterfactual assumption will still give us the result that a large number of women are missing.

The journalist and writer Mara Hvistendahl tells this tale in a gripping 2011 book, *Unnatural Selection*. She vividly documents among other things that the cultural fact of son preference is widespread throughout Asia, Eastern Europe, and elsewhere and traces the ways in which it manifests itself, invariably in ways that are detrimental to women and girls.

In olden times, this cultural preference for boys might manifest itself through female infanticide or the deliberate neglect of female children. The British rulers of colonial India discovered the widespread existence of female infanticide among certain communities in the Rajput warrior caste in western India but weren't successful in stopping the practice. In our modern world though, a preference for boys is much simpler to express and perhaps less morally challenging than infanticide: it's called sex-selective abortion. With the widespread and affordable availability of pre-natal screening, which determines the gender of an unborn child, and the equally widespread availability of abortion, it becomes relatively easy for parents to abort female foetuses, even though the practice is illegal. (To be more precise, Indian law makes gender determination as part of prenatal screening illegal. It's also illegal to abort a foetus citing gender as a reason. Of course, this doesn't mean that these practices don't happen anyway.)

There's corroborating evidence that neglect of girls (making them more likely to die prematurely) may interact with sex selection to worsen the 0–6 sex ratio. Matters look even worse when the sex ratio is parsed by what is known as the 'order of births', that is, looking at the sequence in which boys and girls are born into a family with many children. Research suggests that the ratio of boys to girls jumps as families have more children, conditional on the fact that the earlier births were female. For example, a family that has produced five girls in a row has a very high chance statistically of producing a boy next. That can *only* happen if sex selection is at work, since nature doesn't care how many boys or girls you've already had. Indeed, there's also evidence that excess female mortality in early childhood most strongly affects girls higher up in the birth order. Here's how it might work: a family which desperately wants to have at least one boy might have many girls before that first boy arrives. (In economic jargon, a family's decision to keep having girls until they get their first boy is a type of 'stopping rule'. You might recall we saw stopping rules back in the introductory chapter in the context of situations like dating.) Those girls will then be part of larger families and, therefore, have less access to food, medical care, and household resources, which will be shared among more siblings, and so will be more likely to die young.

But there is another story to tell. The much publicized statistics and media coverage documenting skewed sex ratios in early childhood and the undoubted fact of sex-selective abortion have obscured the possibility that there are other reasons why women might go 'missing'.

Eminent Indian economist Debraj Ray together with his collaborator Siwan Anderson is the first to carefully and systematically explore missing women in different age groups and across different states in India. Ray is an economics professor at New York University and is one of the foremost academic economists working on India. He also has that rare ability to combine high-powered economic theory with sophisticated statistical techniques and apply both to interesting problems and puzzles. And if you were to meet him you might think he was a cool hipster rather than a university professor: no shabby tweeds for him.

Ray and Anderson develop a method to break down, or 'decompose' in statistical jargon, the number of missing women in these different categories. They do this by implementing a version of Sen's counterfactual approach, but applying it separately to every group. For example, for any given age group, they compare male and female mortality with what's observed in the developed world, which they assume to be free of bias against men or women. This assumption lets them compute the missing women in a given year or in a given state rather than just have one single statistic giving us the total number of women missing over time. (Technically, Anderson and Ray are looking at 'flows' of women rather than the total 'stock'. This would be exactly analogous to looking at the flow of investment rather than total stock of capital.)

Anderson and Ray's approach gives us a much finer grained understanding of the problem rather than just baldly saying that a certain number of women are missing. They find that there are more than 2 million women missing in India in a given year. This is broadly consistent with what Sen and others before have found. But the biggest payoff to their painstaking approach are the numbers they get when they dig deeper. Their most striking results are that most of the women who go missing do so as adults rather than at birth or as children. They show that about 12 per cent of women in India are missing at birth: these are presumably missing due to sex selective abortion or infanticide. Another 25 per cent perish in childbirth. But that's still only a little more than a third of the total. Another 18 per cent go missing during their reproductive period, which picks up among other things death during childbirth. But a massive 45 per cent of the total number of missing women go missing in adulthood and older age, something which by definition cannot have anything to do with sex selection.

Looking at these numbers tells us that a focus on sex selective abortion and female mortality in childhood is missing out entirely on factors that lead to higher female mortality among adult women. A statistical decomposition by itself cannot pinpoint the causes of death in older age, but Anderson and Ray offer several suggestive possibilities. These include, for example, some 'manmade' factors such as a greater incidence of violence against women. But they also may include a greater incidence of disease, which could reflect either greater neglect of older women or underlying biological factors. But at this point, without further research on the underlying causes, it's impossible to apportion blame among these various factors.

The other big story coming out of Anderson and Ray's research is that there are important differences in the distribution of missing women by age group across different states. This again is something that's totally obscured if we just focus on one headline national number. They find that it's only Punjab where the majority of missing women are missing at birth: in fact it's as high as 60 per cent of the excess female mortality in that state. This is in line with the extremely high childhood sex ratios reported in Punjab and fits the idea that a high rate of sex-selective abortion is taking place. This is one state where the conventional wisdom seems to hold true: the phenomenon of missing women is driven by sex-selective abortion and reflects the combination of patriarchy and a high income level which makes pre-natal screening and abortion widely available.

Two other states show up as having a majority of their women missing at birth or in childhood (before the age of 15) and it shouldn't surprise you to learn that they're Haryana and Rajasthan. Haryana is a state that was carved out of Punjab after independence and is demographically very similar as well as also being a rich state. Rajasthan, as we know, has had a problem of female infanticide (and now sex-selective abortion) going back for centuries. Anderson and Ray show that if you add up the missing women in these three states, they're only about 15 per cent of the total number of missing women in India.

But for all the other states, the conventional wisdom doesn't hold, and most of the women go missing as adults. Three of the southern states, Kerala, Tamil Nadu, and Andhra Pradesh, have the lowest number of missing women in the country and make up only 10 per cent of the total. The remaining missing women are distributed in different ways around the rest of the country. One group of states (Madhya Pradesh, Maharashtra, Bihar, and Assam) comprise about 37 per cent of the total missing women and they have the highest excess female mortality at all age groups, especially high among adults. And yet another group of states (West Bengal, Orissa, Himachal Pradesh, and Uttar Pradesh), which account for about a third of the total missing women, have relatively low excess female mortality at younger ages but higher mortality at adult ages.

Another way of understanding what's going on is to try the following experiment. Suppose you were to order the states by sex ratio at birth from the most skewed to the least skewed and then you constructed another ordering which shows the percentage of a state's women which are missing, again from the worst to the least bad. Anderson and Ray observe that there would be a very low correlation between the two groups of states: in other words, sex selection is far from being the most important part of the story. The only states which come at or near the top of both lists are Punjab and Haryana and these are indeed the states that form the basis of our received opinion about the problem of missing women in India.

As Anderson and Ray write: 'there's more to missing women than discrepancies in the sex ratio at birth'. Their nuanced conclusion sounds a note which resonates with several themes that we've explored in this chapter: the wide variation in excess female mortality across states and across age groups makes it difficult (and we would add unwise) to provide what they call a 'one-dimensional explanation' for missing women. In other words, 'missing women' does not mean the same thing as women never born.

A single headline splashed across the top of the page doesn't do justice to the complexity of the issues, whether it's the prevalence of HIV, child malnutrition, violence against women, or missing women. The news from India, like India itself, requires us to dig deeper into the story and not stop with the headline.

Notes

Introduction: Mind Games

I

We spoke to Prasanna Sankhe about his 'ISH' watch by telephone on August 12, 2012. Note that here, and hereafter in the book, when we say that 'we' spoke to or communicated with someone, we mean that either one or the other or in some cases both of us spoke to or communicated with that person.

The academic paper on punctuality that we discuss in the text is: Kaushik Basu and Jörgen W. Weibull, 'Punctuality—A Cultural Trait as Equilibrium,' in R. Arnott, R. Kanbur, B. Greenwald, and B. Nalebuff (eds.), *Economics for an Imperfect World: Essays in Honor of Joseph Stiglitz*, MIT Press, Cambridge, 2003.

The classic reference on the collective action problem is: Mancur Olson, *The Logic of Collective Action: Public Goods and the Theory of Groups*, revised edition, Harvard University Press, 1971. The argument that it is the rule of law, not culture, that helps explain Western economic ascendency (including in matters such as public health) over the past half-millennium is made forcefully in the important (and controversial) recent book by Niall Ferguson, *Civilization: The West and the Rest*, Penguin Press, 2011.

The classic paper explaining the economics of the 'QWERTY' keyboard that we mention is by Paul A. David, 'Clio and the Economics of QWERTY', *American Economic Review: Papers and Proceedings*, 1985, volume 75.

II

The report on John Abraham having his fare refused by a Mumbai autorickshaw driver, and his support for Meter Down, was: 'I know how it feels to be refused by autos: John', *Mid-Day*, January 19, 2012. On Meter Down itself and the motivation behind the campaign, see: Sachin Kalbag, 'Solving the auto conundrum', *Mid-Day*, October 11, 2011.

Choosing a mate from among a fixed and known number of candidates that you can rank is a version of the 'secretary problem', itself a classic example of an optimal stopping problem. See, for example: P.R. Freeman, 'The Secretary Problem and its Extensions: A Review', *International Statistical Review*, 1983, volume 51.

Rupa discusses the economics of taxi shortage in Mumbai and probes the underlying reasons here: 'Economics Journal: Stupid Taxi Rules in Mumbai', *Wall Street Journal India Real Time*, August 1, 2012.

III

For more on Priyanka Vadra signalling through her dress choice and other examples of signalling at work, see: Rupa Subramanya, 'Economics Journal: Is Priyanka's Dress Sense Insincere?', *Wall Street Journal India Real Time*, January 23, 2012.

The classic paper on the economics of signalling is: Michael Spence, 'Job Market Signalling', *Quarterly Journal of Economics*, 1973, volume 87. As it happens, Spence shared the 2001 Nobel prize with Joseph Stiglitz and another pioneer in the economics of uncertainty, George Akerlof.

The classic paper on efficiency wages is by Carl Shapiro and Stiglitz, 'Equilibrium Unemployment as a Worker Discipline Device', *American Economic Review*, 1984, volume 74. The corresponding classic on the 'lemons problem' is by (you guessed it) Akerlof, 'The Market for "Lemons": Quality Uncertainty and the Market Mechanism,' *Quarterly Journal of Economics*, 1970, volume 84.

Enough has been written about the global financial crisis to fill many shelves of a library and our discussion in the text is the barest of summaries, meant to illustrate the concepts of moral hazard and adverse selection. One of the best and most accessible treatments is by Raghuram Rajan, *Fault Lines: How Hidden Fractures Still Threaten the World Economy*, Princeton University Press, 2011. Rajan took over from Basu in the middle of 2012 as the Indian government's chief economic adviser.

Chapter 1: A Helping Hand

I

Iris Chang's book on the Nanking massacre is *The Rape of Nanking: The Forgotten Holocaust of World War II*, Basic Books, 1997, reissued 2012.

Yasmin Khan's account of the Partition is *The Great Partition: The Making of India and Pakistan*, Yale University Press, 2007.

There was extensive coverage in the Indian media in the days following the murders of Keenan and Reuben. The facts as presented in the text have been culled from various widely available sources, all of which may be readily found through an internet search. Here's a representative news story: Shiva Devnath, 'Vengeful eve-teaser's gang kills youth, injures two', *Mid-Day*, Mumbai, October 22, 2011. The quotation from Priyanka comes from an interview with Rinkita Gurav, 'Hope men learn from Keenan's courage', *Mid-Day*, Mumbai, November 3, 2011.

For stories similar to Keenan and Reuben, here are two news reports, from two different cities, selected more or less at random. The first describes a 17-year-old girl from Bangalore who died when a wall collapsed on her. As the reporter puts it: 'Yes, the girl could have survived had the scores of bystanders acted with alacrity and either pulled out the girl or alerted the fire brigade immediately, instead of remaining mute spectators.' See Arun Dev, 'It was public apathy that killed Sanjana Singh', *Daily News and Analysis*, Bangalore, June 4, 2010. The second describes a university student in Delhi being beaten to death, and his friend severely injured, while passersby didn't intervene to help. The reporter comments that: 'Delhiites once again showed a bizarre display of apathy towards the victims of a crime.' See Karan Pratap Singh, 'He screamed for help, but no one came forward even as his friend bled to death', *Hindustan Times*, New Delhi, November 29, 2011.

Again, the tragedy in Foshan was widely reported in the international media. Here's a representative example: Keith B. Richburg, 'Toddler in China hit by 2 vehicles, then ignored, dies', *Washington Post*, October 21, 2011.

II

Richard Dawkins' classic book that brought Darwin's theory of natural selection to a wide public is *The Selfish Gene*, Oxford University Press, 1976.

The debate about cooperation and altruism in the animal kingdom has been reopened by Edward O. Wilson in *The Social Conquest of Earth*, Liveright, 2012. We also draw upon Jonah Lehrer, 'Kin and Kind', *New Yorker*, March 5, 2002, especially in our illustration of the concept using the vampire bat.

For J.B.S. Haldane's work on evolutionary biology, his classic early article is 'Population genetics', *New Biology*, 1955, volume 18. W.D. Hamilton's famous pair of articles are 'The genetical evolution of social behaviour', parts I and II, *Journal of Theoretical Biology*, 1964, volume 7.

Haldane's India connection is discussed by Ramachandra Guha in *An Anthropologist Among the Marxists and Other Essays*, Permanent Black, New Delhi, 2001. See the chapter entitled 'The Other Side of the Raj: Mira, Spratt, Elwin and Haldane.'

On reciprocal altruism, the classic early paper is Robert L. Trivers, 'The Evolution of Reciprocal Altruism', *Quarterly Review of Biology*, 1971, volume 46.

The article we refer to is Martin A. Nowak, Corina E. Tarnita, and Edward O. Wilson, 'The evolution of eusociality', *Nature*, 2010, volume 466.

III

An important contribution to the literature we mention is Ingela Alger and Jörgen W. Weibull, 'A generalization of Hamilton's rule—Love others how much?', *Journal of Theoretical Biology*, 2012, volume 299.

The seminal article on 'social preferences' is Gary S. Becker, 'A Theory of Social Interactions', *Journal of Political Economy*, 1974, volume 82. The first application of Becker's theory to the problem of altruism is William M. Landes and Richard A. Posner, 'Salvors, Finders, Good Samaritans, and Other Rescuers: An Economic Study of Law and Altruism', *Journal of Legal Studies*, 1978, volume 7. See also Landes and Posner, 'Altruism in Law and Economics', *American Economic Review: Papers and Proceedings*, 1978, volume 68. This latter article is also the source of our reference later in the text to Landes and Posner commenting on Good Samaritan laws.

The Peng Yu case was widely covered by the international media. A representative news story is: Adam Minter, 'China's Infamous "Good Samaritan" Case Gets a New Ending', *Bloomberg View*, January 18, 2012. The case is rather murky as some sources suggest that Peng confessed to the crime or might have colluded with the woman who sued him. A representative Indian example may be found in Vijay V. Singh, 'Mumbai's good samaritans get a boost', *Times of India*, Mumbai, July 30, 2012.

The classic psychological experiment on altruistic behaviour is by John M. Darley and C. Daniel Batson, 'From Jerusalem to Jericho: A Study of Situational and Dispositional Variables in Helping Behavior', *Journal of Personality and Social Psychology*, 1973, volume 27.

IV

A great book on the economics of bargaining and strategic behaviour, with many real world examples, is by Thomas C. Schelling, *The Strategy of Conflict*, Harvard University Press, 1980.

The idea that market failure must be weighed against government failure, producing a general scepticism about the government's ability to correct market failure without actually making things worse, is a recurring theme in the economics of the Chicago School. See in particular George J. Stigler, 'The theory of economic regulation', *Bell Journal of Economics and Management*, 1971, volume 2. See also Posner, 'The Social Costs of Monopoly and Regulation', *Journal of Political Economy*, 1975, volume 83.

Our discussion in the text has introduced the concept of market failure as driven by transaction costs. This is a classic 'Chicago School' approach to the issue. The seminal contribution to this way of thinking is by Ronald Coase, who won a Nobel Prize in Economics in 1991. The more conventional, textbook approach, which you might call the 'Cambridge School' approach (whether Cambridge in the UK or Harvard and MIT in the US), is to frame market failure as being driven by an 'externality', something that one person does which has an effect on another, that isn't captured or 'internalized' by the market system.

The article by R.H. Coase that we mention, which shows that market failure is rooted in transaction costs, is 'The Problem of Social Cost', *Journal of Law and Economics*, 1960, volume 3. The conventional approach which grounds market failure in externalities may be found in any standard principles of economics textbook. See, for example, N. Gregory Mankiw, *Principles of Economics*, sixth edition, South-Western College Publishing, 2011.

V

This section draws on two separate telephone conversations we had with Piyush Tewari, on January 12 and 28, 2012, and on subsequent email exchanges.

The statistic that 80 per cent of victims don't receive the treatment they need within the first hour is widely quoted and readily available in news coverage of roadside accidents in India. Our specific source is the website of Piyush Tewari's NGO, Save Life Foundation.

Social psychologists speak of the 'bystander effect'. It's often called the 'Kitty Genovese effect', after a notorious and much studied episode in New York City in 1964, in which a woman was stabbed and then sexually assaulted and left to die on the street. The fact that an apparently large number of bystanders did nothing led to outrage in the media, similar to what we've seen recently in India and China. The story has been subsequently much debated and the original version of events challenged. There is a concise discussion in Steven D. Levitt and Stephen J. Dubner, *Superfreakonomics*, Penguin Books, 2010, chapter 3.

The Templeton Foundation debate on the free market and morality that we mention, may be found at their website. Vivek has written an op-ed on this subject, 'Can capitalism and morality be friends?', *Hindustan Times*, New Delhi, February 4, 2012. An academic review of the debate from a sociological perspective may be found in Marion Fourcade and Kieran Healy, 'Moral Views of Market Society', *Annual Review of Sociology*, 2007, volume 33.

The debate in China began almost immediately after the tragedy in Foshan and found its way into much international coverage of the incident. See, for example, Michael Wines, 'Bystanders' Neglect of Injured Toddler Sets Off Soul-Searching on Websites in China', *New York Times*, October 19, 2011. See also Charles Burton, 'China's hit-and-run morality', *Globe and Mail*, Toronto, October 20, 2011. On the debate in India, see, for example, Barkha Dutt, 'The victim syndrome', *Hindustan Times*, New Delhi, November 12, 2011.

The 'warm glow' effect was first introduced into economics by James Andreoni, 'Impure Altruism and Donations to Public Goods:

A Theory of Warm-Glow Giving', *Economic Journal*, 1990, volume 100.

The incentives offered to Good Samaritans by the state of Maharashtra are discussed in: 'State to reward Good Samaritans', *Daily News and Analysis*, Mumbai, July 20, 2012.

Chapter 2: The Human Factor

I

Our discussion of the 1962 war draws heavily on Ramachandra Guha, 'Jawaharlal Nehru and China: A Study in Failure?', Harvard-Yenching Institute Working Paper Series, 2011. The paper is based on a lecture given at Harvard and is available for download from the institute's website.

The August 1961 quotation from Nehru as recounted by Shashi Tharoor, and our subsequent references to him in the text, are drawn from, *Nehru: The Invention of India*, Penguin Books, 2003, chapter 9.

The quotation from Nehru about living in an artificial atmosphere is much cited and widely reproduced. See, for example, Fareed Zakaria, *The Post American World and the Rise of the Rest*, Penguin Books, 2009, p. 149.

11

The Mega Millions lottery received a great deal of press coverage in March 2012 in the lead up to the huge jackpot. As a representative example, see: David Beasley, 'World record $640 million lottery drawing set for Friday night', *Reuters*, Atlanta, March 30, 2012. For an economic analysis see Steven Levitt and Stephen Dubner's 'Freakonomics' blogpost of March 30, 2012. Our discussion of the Canadian lottery and a comparison of the odds of winning it is taken from 'Lotteries: What are the odds?', *CBC News*, November 9, 2009.

Our discussion of the lottery business in India draws on Shantanu Guha Ray, 'The Trader of Shadow Fortunes', *Tehelka Magazine*, February 13, 2010.

For our discussion of Delhi's road safety week, we draw on Nikita Garia, 'Delhi Traffic Police to Give Money to Good Pedestrians', *Wall Street Journal India Real Time*, January 10, 2012. The quotation from the police commissioner is taken from Ananya Bhardwaj, 'Use foot-overbridge, win Rs 5,000: Cops to reward pedestrians', *Indian Express*, New Delhi, February 16, 2012.

The data on traffic fatalities in Delhi are taken from Annex XVIII of *Road Accidents in India: 2011*, published by the Government of India's Transport Research Wing, Ministry of Road Transport and Highways, released June 2012.

III

Data on fatalities from crossing the railway tracks in India are taken from 'Report of High Level Safety Review Committee', published by the Government of India's Ministry of Railways, released February 2012.

IV

For a discussion on cognitive psychology and behavioural economics, see Daniel Kahneman, *Thinking, Fast and Slow*, Allen Lane (Penguin Group), 2011.

For the Rubicon theory of war, see Dominic Johnson and Dominic Tierney, 'The Rubicon Theory of War: How the Path to Conflict Reaches the Point of No Return', *International Security*, 2011, volume 36. Johnson's book is *Overconfidence in War: The Havoc and Glory of Positive Illusions*, Harvard University Press, 2004. The quotation from Tierney is in an email to us dated March 26, 2012. The book by Eliot A. Cohen and John Gooch is *Military Misfortunes: The Anatomy of Failure in War*, Anchor Books, 1991.

V

See Abhijit Banerjee and Esther Duflo, *Poor Economics: A Radical Rethinking of the Way to Fight Global Poverty*, PublicAffairs, 2011.

For the particular cognitive challenges that the poor face, see Marianne Bertrand, Sendhil Mullainathan, and Eldar Shafir, 'A

Behavioral Economics View of Poverty', *American Economic Review: Papers and Proceedings*, 2004, volume 94. The work by Mullianathan, Shafir, and Anandi Mani on sugarcane farmers in Tamil Nadu is as yet unpublished.

VI

See Richard Thaler and Cass Sunstein, *Nudge: Improving Decisions About Health, Wealth and Happiness*, Penguin Books, 2008, revised 2009.

For the claim that Sunstein 'wielded enormous power' in the White House during his stint in the Obama administration, see: John M. Broder, 'Powerful Shaper of U.S. Rules Quits, With Critics in Wake', *New York Times*, August 4, 2012.

Our discussion of the work by FinalMile is based on a conversation with Biju Dominic and members of his team at their offices in Mumbai on February 17, 2012. See also two articles by Samanth Subramanian, 'Mind games to stop death on the tracks', *Mint*, January 6, 2010, and 'Train!', *Boston Globe*, May 8, 2011.

On the nudges by traffic police we describe, see: Meenakshi Mahadevan, 'Chennai cops use gory ads to promote helmet use', *CNN-IBN*, October 26, 2010; and Yogesh Sadhwani, 'Speed thrills? These cars will change you', *Mumbai Mirror*, January 2, 2012.

Chapter 3: What If...?

I

The data on traffic fatalities are taken from *Road Accidents in India: 2011*, published by the Government of India's Transport Research Wing, Ministry of Road Transport and Highways, released June 2012.

The details on Delhi's fines for failing to wear a seatbelt are from the Delhi Traffic Police's own website.

Our discussion of automobile safety regulation in the US draws on the classic paper by Sam Peltzman, 'The Effects of Automobile Safety Regulation', *Journal of Political Economy*, 1975, volume 83. Amazingly, Peltzman's paper appeared in the same issue as the classic paper by Richard Posner on the social costs of regulation, that we referred to in our chapter on apathy vs. altruism.

The paper we cite is: Alma Cohen and Rajeev Dehejia, 'The Effect of Automobile Insurance and Accident Liability Laws on Traffic Fatalities', *Journal of Law and Economics*, 2004, volume 47.

The study by Dinesh Mohan is 'Seat Belt Law and Road Traffic Injuries in Delhi, India', *Journal of the Eastern Asia Society for Transportation Studies*, 2010, volume 8.

For the effects of helmet use in professional sports, see, for example: Alan Schwarz, 'A Case Against Helmets in Lacrosse', *New York Times*, February 17, 2011.

For a discussion of the one child policy in China and the family planning drive in India, see: Mara Hvistendahl, *Unnatural Selection: Choosing Boys over Girls, and the Consequences of a World Full of Men*, PublicAffairs, New York, 2011.

II

The *Hindustan Times* and CNN-IBN survey was reported in: Abhijit Patnaik, 'Will the honest netas, please stand up', Hindustan Times Leadership Summit, December 2, 2011. The second survey we refer to is *State of Democracy in South Asia*, Oxford University Press, 2008. See also Peter R. deSouza, Suhas Palshikar, and Yogendra Yadav, 'Surveying South Asia', *Journal of Democracy*, 2008, volume 19.

The quotation from Lee Kwan Yew appears in the *Economist*, August 27, 1994. The quotation from Mahathir Mohammed is taken from his keynote address at the Hindustan Times Leadership Summit, 2011 we've just mentioned. It was widely cited in the press. Here's a representative example: 'Less democracy better for India, says Mahathir', *Hindustan Times*, New Delhi, December 2, 2011.

The quotation from Indira Gandhi expressing doubts about democracy is from Ramachandra Guha, *An Anthropologist Among the Marxists and Other Essays*, Permanent Black, New Delhi, 2001, p. 186.

Our discussion of Indira Gandhi's Emergency draws on Ramachandra Guha, *India After Gandhi: The History of the World's Largest Democracy*, McMillan, 2007, chapter 22.

The quotation from Shashi Tharoor is from *India: From Midnight to the Millennium and Beyond*, revised and updated, Penguin Books, 2007, p. 234.

The study by William Easterly is 'Benevolent Autocrats', August 2011. This as yet unpublished study is available from Easterly's website.

III

The research we refer to in by Laura Cray and her co-authors is: 'From What *Might* Have Been to What *Must* Have Been: Counterfactual Thinking Creates Meaning', *Journal of Personality and Social Psychology*, 2010, volume 98.

Robert Fogel's research that we refer to is, *Railroads and American Economic Growth: Essays in Econometric History*, Johns Hopkins University Press, 1964.

On counterfactual history, see, Niall Ferguson, editor, *Virtual History: Alternatives and Counterfactuals*, Picador Books, 1997.

For Niall Ferguson on the 'benign' British Empire, see *Empire: How Britain Made the Modern World*, Allen Lane (Penguin Group), 2003.

Dave Donaldson, an economics professor at M.I.T., has studied the beneficial impacts of British-build railways on reducing transportation costs and so boosting trade and income in colonial India. Note, of course, that this doesn't by itself answer a counterfactual question, since we don't know if India would have anyway gotten a rail network without the British. See, Dave Donaldson, 'Railroads of the Raj: Estimating the Impact of Transportation Infrastructure', MIT Economics Department Working Paper, October 2010.

The address by Prime Minister Manmohan Singh in accepting an honorary doctorate from Oxford University was on July 8, 2005. It's been widely reproduced, including by *The Hindu* newspaper. The quotation from Mohan Bhagwat is from 'India was better off under British rule: Mohan Bhagwat', *Times of India*, Nashik, February 22, 2012. The quotation from the Hindu ideologue cited is from a private conversation and was not intended by him for publication.

On the debate between Amartya Sen and Niall Ferguson in the *New Republic*, see Amartya Sen, 'Imperial Illusions: India, Britain, and the wrong lessons', the *New Republic*, December 31, 2007. The rejoinder from Ferguson, 'Don't use me as a straw man, Professor Sen!', appeared on February 15, 2008, as did Sen's reply, 'Disputations: More on "Imperial Illusions".' Sens's first sentence is delicious: 'I'm grateful to Niall Ferguson, whose insightful writings I admire, for bothering to respond to my essay.' He then proceeds to a thorough dissection.

For the research on spending patterns on education in British India, see Latika Chaudhary, 'Determinants of Primary Schooling in British India', *Journal of Economic History*, 2009, volume 69.

For Lakshmi Iyer's research see, 'Direct vs. Indirect Colonial rule in India: Long-Term consequences', *Review of Economics and Statistics*, 2010, volume 92.

The article by Jabez T. Sutherland is 'The New Nationalist Movement in India', which appeared in the October 1908 issue of the *Atlantic* magazine. It's archived on their website. On Baroda, see, for example, Niranjan Rajadhyaksha, 'Returning to the age of Ranade', *Mint*, June 29, 2012.

The 'Star Trek' episode we mention in the text is 'The City on the Edge of Forever', season 1, episode 28, first broadcast on April 6, 1967.

Chapter 4: Heads or Tails?

I

The A.C. Neilson poll was widely publicized in advance of the election. For more details see: 'Poll predicts 300 seats for NDA', *The Hindu*, March 28, 2004; and 'NDA will bag 287–300 seats: Opinion poll,' Rediff.com, March 27, 2004. On the importance of polls in the 2004 election, see Soutik Biswas, 'Indian exit polls steal the show', *BBC News*, May 12, 2004.

On the BJP's admission that 'India Shining' backfired, see 'BJP admits "India Shining" error', *BBC News*, May 28, 2004.

A few analysts did get it right in the immediate aftermath of the election, including Arvind Panagariya, an international affairs professor at Columbia University and columnist for the *Economic Times*. Arvind Panagariya's piece bucking the conventional wisdom that we refer to is: 'High growth, low votes', *BBC News*, March 27, 2009.

We spoke to Yogendra Yadav by telephone on February 24 and 25, 2012. He's written extensively on polling, elections, and Indian democracy. On the 2004 election specifically, see: 'The Elusive Mandate of 2004', *Economic and Political Weekly*, December 18, 2004.

II

TrustLaw Survey, 'The world's most dangerous countries for women', June 15, 2011 is available at their website.

Philip Tetlock's landmark book is *Expert Political Judgement: How Good Is It? How Can We Know?*, Princeton University Press, 2005. For a condensed version of his argument, see Dan Gardner and Philip Tetlock, 'Overcoming our aversion to acknowledging our ignorance', *CATO Unbound*, July 11, 2011.

The study on the Olympics is Daniel K.N. Johnson and Ayfer Ali, 'A Tale of Two Seasons: Participation and Medal Counts at the Summer and Winter Olympic Games', *Social Science Quarterly*, 2004, volume 85. The takedown by Roger Pielke, Jr, is on the 'Freakonomics' blogpage, March 27, 2012.

Dan Gardner's book which popularizes Tetlock's research and gives many examples is *Future Babble*, Virgin Books, London, 2011.

III

The case that our life is governed by randomness is made by Nassim Nicholas Taleb, *Fooled by Randomness: The Hidden Role of Chance in Life and in the Markets*, Penguin Books, 2007.

The commentary on the UP election spanned the three theories and as we noted, are well-represented in the media analysis that followed the election results. Here was Rupa's take: 'Economics Journal: Identity Politics vs. Development Politics', *Wall Street Journal India Real Time*, March 7, 2012. Columnists who argued the pro-development theory are: Pratap Bhanu Mehta, 'Mandate for a dream', *Indian Express*, March 7, 2012; and Arvind Panagariya, 'UP election shows that reforms, not the Gandhi name, will win future polls', *Economic Times*, March 21, 2012. Sadanand Dhume, 'India Still Privileges Princelings', *Wall Street Journal*, March 15, 2012 argues for a mix of identity politics and anti-incumbency.

IV

The quotation from Patrick French is on p. 74 of his book, *India: An Intimate Biography of 1.2 Billion People*, Allen Lane (Penguin Group), 2011.

See Malcolm Gladwell, *Outliers: The Story of Success*, Penguin Books, 2008.

The study by Sean Rehaag on refugee claims is 'The Luck of the Draw? Judicial Review of Refugee Determinations in the Federal Court of Canada (2005–2010)', forthcoming in *Queen's Law Journal*.

For details on the LinkedIn study reported on here, see Tiffany Hsu: '84% of professionals believe in career luck: LinkedIn Survey', *Los Angeles Times*, March 13, 2012. You can find a report on the Indian counterpart study here: '79% of Indian professionals believe in career luck', *Business Standard*, March 14, 2012.

Shekhar Aiyar and Rodney Ramcharan's study on cricket is : 'What Can International Cricket Teach Us About the Role of Luck in Labor Markets?', IMF Working Paper, WP/10/225, October 2010. They wrote a non-technical summary in 'A Lucky Start', *Finance & Development*, 2010, volume 47. Aiyar shared his views with us by email on March 25, 2012.

Chapter 5: Mythical or Modern?

I

Recently, economists have begun to study the impact of history (understood broadly to include institutions, culture, religion, etc.) on economic outcomes. See, for example, Nathan Nunn, 'The Importance of History for Economic Development', *Annual Review of Economics*, 2009, volume 1. See also Alberto Bisin and Thierry Verdier, 'The Economics of Cultural Transmission and Socialization', National Bureau of Economic Research, Working Paper 16512, November 2010.

There's a gripping account of the discovery of treasure at the Sri Padmanabhaswamy temple in Jake Halpern, 'The Secret of the Temple: A Reporter at Large', *New Yorker*, April 30, 2012.

For a report on the spike in gold prices before Akshaya Tritiya, see, for example, 'Gold buying slows after Akshaya Tritiya', *Reuters*, Mumbai, April 25, 2012. The Macquarie study on the Indian demand for gold is: Tanvee Gupta Jain, 'Macro Mantra: India's fatal attraction', November 29, 2011. The press release by the World Gold Council quoting Ajay Mitra is dated May 3, 2012.

II

The study by Gabriele M. Lepori is 'Dark Omens in the Sky: Do Superstitious Beliefs Affect Investment Decisions?', Copenhagen Business School Working Paper, June 2009. Our discussion of eclipses in Greek and Roman mythology also draws on this study.

The study on the 'lucky ball' is: Lysann Damisch et al., 'Keep Your Fingers Crossed! How Superstition Improves Performance', *Psychological Science*, May 2010.

III

The study on Chinese numerology and the Vancouver housing market is: Nicole M. Fortin, Andrew J. Hill, and Jeff Huang, 'Superstition in the Housing Market', University of British Columbia Working Paper, January 2011.

As we suggest , it was widely reported in advance that the starting date and time of the Beijing Summer Olympics were selected because it was auspicious. See, for example, 'Lucky number for Chinese Olympics', *BBC News*, November 5, 2004. However, for the denial by the American television executive, see Bill Carter, 'On TV, Timing is Everything at the Olympics', *New York Times*, August 25, 2008.

Our data and analysis of the effects of 'Hinoeuma' in Japan are drawn from Hideo Akabayashi, 'Who suffered from the superstition in the marriage market? The case of Hinoeuma in Japan', Keio University Working Paper, December 26, 2006.

The study on Dragon kids is: Noel D. Johnson and John V.C. Nye, 'Does fortune favor dragons?', *Journal of Economic Behavior & Organization*, 2011, volume 78.

The new story of assisted reproduction clinics is by Shirley S. Wang, 'Having a Baby in Year of the Dragon is Too Lucky to be Left to Chance', *Wall Street Journal*, January 23, 2012. The story about increased early childhood spending in Hong Kong is by Juliana Liu, 'Dragon babies spark spending spree', BBC News, January 27, 2012.

IV

We spoke to Devdutt Pattanaik in Mumbai on July 4, 2012.

Our reference to Mircea Eliade is from *Myths, Dreams, and Mysteries*, Harper & Row, 1967. The most famous and accessible of his many books is *The Sacred and the Profane: The Nature of Religion*, Harcourt Brace, 1961.

The term 'Washington consensus', referring to a set of economic policies ostensibly promoted by the US government and international financial institutions based in Washington, DC, notably the World Bank and International Monetary Fund, was coined by the economist John Williamson in 1989. See: Williamson, 'What Washington Means by Policy Reform', in Williamson, ed., *Latin American Readjustment: How Much has Happened*, Washington, Institute for International Economics, 1989.

Much has been written on the global financial crisis, and our discussion in the text is necessarily cursory, focusing as it does on the cultural dimension we wish to highlight. We also cannot do justice to the complex and unresolved debates on the exact causes of the crisis and to what extent lax (or faulty) regulation and global capital flows may be blamed. For a great, balanced overview of the crisis, its causes, and aftermath, see, for example: Raghuram Rajan, *Fault Lines: How Hidden Fractures Still Threaten the World Economy*, Princeton University Press, 2011.

Rupa has written on the differences between charitable giving in India and the West. See 'Economics Journal: Why Charity is Different in India', *Wall Street Journal India Real Time*, July 11, 2012. The Bain & Co. study, 'India Philanthropy Report', was released on June 29, 2011 and is available from the company's website. Oxfam India's 2011 Annual Report, 'New Strategy Takes Root', is likewise available from their website.

The study using Canadian data, which we mention, is: James Andreoni et al., 'Diversity and Donations: The Effect of Religious and Ethnic Diversity on Charitable Giving', National Bureau of Economic Research Working Paper 17618, November 2011.

The large value of the trust that Sathya Sai Baba left upon his death was widely reported. See, for example, 'Sathya Sai Baba, Guru With Millions of Followers, Dies at 84', *Associated Press*, April 24, 2011.

V

For a riveting account of the year leading up to India's independence, see: Dominique Lapierre and Larry Collins, *Freedom at Midnight*, Vikas Publishing, 2009.

Lord Mountbatten credited Prime Minister Nehru for his 'ingenious' solution in 'Reflections on the Transfer of Power and Jawaharlal Nehru', a lecture he gave to the Nehru Memorial Trust at Cambridge University on November 14, 1968. The lecture is available at the trust's website.

On the question of who should get credit for coming up with the midnight solution, see H.V.R. Iyengar, 'Recalling the historic midnight scene', *The Hindu*, August 15, 2007.

Chapter 6: News from India

I

The US government report is 'The Next Wave of HIV/AIDS: Nigeria, Ethopia, Russia, India, and China', prepared by the National Intelligence Council, Report ICA 2002–04d and was released September 2002.

For the adverse reaction by India's health minister, see: 'Gates on India Aids mission', *BBC News*, November 11, 2002. On Bill Clinton's claim that India would become the epicentre of the AIDS epidemic, see: 'India 'Overestimates' HIV/Aids', *BBC News*, December 13, 2006.

The selection of news headlines on HIV/AIDS we present in the text were found by searching a standard library database. They're only a tiny selection of the literally hundreds or thousands of such headlines. Likewise, the Google search is from Google Trends and simply involves searching under the key words 'HIV' and 'AIDS'.

The study by Lalit Dandona et al. is: 'Is the HIV burden in India being overestimated?', *BMC Public Health*, 2006, volume 6.

The UN's admission that it had overstated the number of HIV cases was widely reported. Here's a representative news story: Donald G. McNeil Jr, 'UN to Say It Overstated H.I.V Cases by Millions', *New York Times*, November 20, 2007.

The updated numbers on HIV/AIDS incidence for India are from: Prabhat Jha et al., 'HIV mortality and infection in India: estimates from nationally representative mortality survey of 1.1 million homes', *British Medical Journal*, 2010, volume 340.

On the debate over the incidence of child malnutrition in India and the media coverage, see Rupa Subramanya's piece: 'Economics Journal: Is India as Malnourished as Data Suggest?', *Wall Street Journal India Real Time*, June 20, 2012. See also: Subramanya, 'Economics Journal: Why Gujarat's Hunger Stats May Mislead', *Wall Street Journal India Real Time*, September 5, 2012.

As we say , Arvind Panagariya's research on child malnutrition is as yet unpublished, although he shared a copy with us electronically on June 15, 2012. A version of the research, under the title 'The Myth of Child Malnutrition in India', was presented at a Columbia University conference under the aegis of the Programme on Indian Economic Policies, 'India: Reforms, Economic Transformation and the Socially Disadvantaged', September 20–22, 2012. He's also written on the subject here: 'The child malnutrition myth', *Times of India*, October 1, 2011. The classic academic study on puzzles around nutrition in India is: Angus Deaton and Jean Drèze, 'Food and Nutrition in India: Facts and Interpretations,' *Economic & Political Weekly*, February 14, 2009.

The UN Human Development Report, 2011 is entitled, 'Sustainability and Equity: A Better Future for All', and is available from the United Nations Development Programme (UNDP).

On the debate whether the drug companies influenced the WHO in declaring the swine flu a pandemic, see: Helen Epstein, 'Flu Warning: Beware the Drug Companies!', *New York Review of Books*, May 12, 2011.

II

Government of India statistics on crime are published by the National Crime Records Bureau of the Ministry of Home Affairs. The calculation on the rate of increase is our own based on the data.

The data from UN Women that we cite in the text is from a March 2011 report entitled 'Violence against Women Prevalence Data: Surveys by Country'.

The TrustLaw report, 'The best and worst G20 countries for women', was released in 2012. The report and supporting documents are available from the website. The Reuters story we refer to is: Nita Bhalla, 'India advances, but many women still trapped in dark ages', TrustLaw, June 13, 2012. Here are two representative tweets by this journalist (whose Twitter handle is @nitabhalla). The first tweet reads in part: 'if you look at security, yes. women in saudi not allowed out without chaperon, so less cases of rape reported.' The second reads in part: 'also, we must remember while women are restricted in saudi, they still by and large have the right to life.'

We did reach out to TrustLaw Women by email for clarification on the rationale for their methodology of the earlier survey we studied but all we received was an uninformative boilerplate reply on April 10, 2012.

The study we refer to on crimes against women and their political representation is: Lakshmi Iyer et al., 'The Power of Political Voice: Women's Political Representation and Crime in India', Harvard Business School, Working Paper 11-092, July 2011.

The study by Jean Drèze and Reetika Khera is 'Crime, Gender, and Society in India: Insights from Homicide Data', *Population and Development Review*, 2000, volume 26. Drèze and Khera confirmed to us by email on January 8 and 9, 2012, respectively, that they have not pursued this research further.

III

Our account of Mary Kom's life and career draws on Rahul Bhattacharya, 'India's Shot at Gold', *Intelligent Life*, July/August 2012.

We refer to Abhinav Bindra's memoir. The book is: *A Shot At History*, Harper Collins India, 2011.

The newspaper coverage of Mary Kom that we refer to in the text is as follows: *Times of India*, Mumbai, May 19, 2012, p. 26; *Dainik Bhaskar*, Delhi, May 19, 2012, p. 12; *Indian Express*, Mumbai, May 19, 2012, p. 19; *Daily News and Analysis*, Mumbai, May 19, 2012, p. 16; and *Daily News and Analysis*, Mumbai, May 20, 2012, p. 21. Our reference to the *Sangai Express* draws on their web edition.

For the argument we draw on on biased reading of balanced news, see: Cass R. Sunstein, 'Breaking Up the Echo', *New York Times*, September 18, 2012.

On the negativity bias in news reporting, we draw on Dan Gardner's post on his blogpage, 'Why good news is an oxymoron', October 22, 2011.

IV

The 2011 Census of India is produced by the Government of India's Ministry of Home Affairs and is also available from their website.

Amartya Sen's classic articles on the problem of missing women are: 'More Than 100 Million Women Are Missing', *New York Review of Books*, December 20, 1990; and 'Missing Women', *British Medical Journal*, 1992, volume 304.

Mara Hvistendahl's book on the skewed sex ratio is *Unnatural Selection: Choosing Boys over Girls, and the Consequences of a World Full of Men*, PublicAffairs, New York, 2011.

The study by Siwan Anderson and Debraj Ray is: 'The Age Distribution of Missing Women in India', New York University Working Paper, March 2012. Anderson and Ray also provide a review of the large literature on sex selection and missing women, on which we draw as well in our discussion of what the research has to say.

Acknowledgements

A book such as this wouldn't have been possible without the superb academic scholarship that we draw on. We'd like to thank all of the scholars whose work we refer to, as well as the many others who are working on improving our understanding of India through painstaking and methodical research. Specifically, we'd like to thank the various people we spoke to as we were working through individual chapters. Without the benefit of their many penetrating observations and insights, the book would have been much the poorer.

Many people we've spoken to both during the course of writing this book and indeed over the years, individually or together, have helped shape our understanding of the Indian reality, from politics to economics and history to culture—with special gratitude to Arvind Panagariya and Ashutosh Varshney for many enlightening and lively conversations. That understanding, we hope, finds expression in this volume. It goes without saying that the conclusions we draw, and the arguments we make, are our own, and don't necessarily accord with the views of anyone we've spoken to, nor indeed of other scholars and analysts, both those whose work we know and those who may be unknown to us.

For fostering our journalistic writing and giving us the space and encouragement in which to explore our ideas, we'd like to thank our respective editors: Paul Beckett, India bureau chief of the *Wall Street Journal*, who gave Rupa her first crack and has been a great source of support ever since; and Heather Timmons, editor of the *New York Times India Ink*, who's been an amazing editor and source of ideas and inspiration for Vivek. Rupa also wants to thank all of the great folks at *WSJ India* and *India Real Time*, in particular, Will Davies who's been a brilliant editor. Vivek especially wants to thank Lydia Polgreen, a former *Times* India correspondent, who first suggested that he should write for *India Ink*, and Vikas Bajaj, the *Times* Mumbai correspondent, for many great conversations. This book couldn't possibly have been written without the training ground we received writing for these great newspapers, to which we owe our thanks. And we would be remiss if we did not acknowledge our readers, from whom we have learned so much.

We would also like to thank our many friends, fellow writers, academics, and journalists, in India and elsewhere, for the many informal seminars that took place over dinner and at people's homes, from which we've learned much. In this electronic age, we owe thanks to our many virtual friends in the world of Twitter and Facebook, only some of whom we've met in real life and the many writers and bloggers in the social media who provide bracing alternatives to the mainstream narratives and have thus deepened our understanding.

The support of Meru Gokhale, editorial director of Random House India, who invited us to write this book, and insisted, to our initial horror, that we write it together, has been immense. We owe thanks to Patrick French, for suggesting the idea of the book, and starting us thinking on it. Without that initial spark, this book would never have been conceived, to say nothing of even being written. Thanks are also due to Faiza Sultan Khan, RHI's editor-at-large, whose work with us on the manuscript has greatly improved whatever literary merits this book may possess.

Sarah Singh has been a great friend and well-wisher; we can't imagine our year in Delhi in 2007–08 without the many evenings spent in her company. In Ottawa, where Vivek teaches, we can't imagine how we could possibly have survived without the friendship and intellectual companionship of Mathieu Courville. Vivek wants to thank his great professors at Columbia, in particular Jagdish Bhagwati and Robert Mundell, who helped shape his scholarly understanding of economics. While acknowledging teachers, Vivek especially wants to thank Robert Anderson, the late Stan Clarke, and Franz Szabo, who made an indelible mark on his intellectual and personal development.

Rupa would like to thank Alison Rehner for her nurturing friendship and helping put her on this path. Steven Davis intervened at a critical time in Rupa's life and without the help he offered, she wouldn't be where she is now.

Our journey would never have begun if not for the love,

encouragement, and support of our respective set of parents. We owe a special thanks to Rajeev, who's encouraged us throughout the process of writing this book. Last but not least, we'd like to thank each other: it truly wouldn't have happened without your tolerance, patience, and good will!

Vivek Dehejia and Rupa Subramanya
Mumbai, India

August 2012

Vivek Dehejia is an economics professor at Carleton University in Ottawa, Canada, and a columnist for *Mint*. Vivek is from Mumbai and at present lives between Ottawa and Mumbai.

Rupa Subramanya is an economist, analyst, and writer. Previously she was a columnist for *Wall Street Journal India*. At present she is editor at large for *Swarajya* and a regular contributor to *Foreign Policy*. Rupa is from Bangalore and at present lives in Mumbai.

A Note on the Type

Sabon is the name of an old-style serif typeface designed by the German-born typographer and designer Jan Tschichold (1902–74) in the period 1964–67. A distinguishing feature of the typeface was that the roman, italic, and bold weights all occupy the same width when typeset—an unusual feature, but this meant that the typeface then only required one set of copyfitting data (rather than three) when compositors had to estimate the length of a text prior to actual typesetting (a common practice before computer-assisted typesetting).

